To Kathy & Fred —

Risk well

and Thrive!

THE POWER OF RISK
ENDORSEMENTS

In *The Power of Risk* Jim McCormick balances logic, reason and passion as he presents a strategic plan for smart risk taking. His plan gives readers the perspective they need to courageously take hold of every opportunity presented to them. It is the first work I've seen which actually goes beyond gut instinct, and emotional motivation, to help a person move past their perceived risk tolerance when they discover their true risk tolerance.

> — DAN BRODSKY-CHENFELD
> 16 time National Champion and 8 time
> World Champion in Formation Skydiving
> Author – *Playing to Win*

Jim McCormick's book is a must read for anyone wanting to get more out of life! You'll find tools that are simple to understand, easy to implement, and produce results. I've taken more than my fair share of risks in life and this book inspired me to immediately increase my Risk Quotient even more.

> — DEAN HOHL
> Leadership Expert
> Author – *Rangers Lead the Way*

Jim McCormick has created a set of tools that can profoundly change your life by removing the most limiting factor of all — the ones you impose.

> — GREG HARTLEY
> Human Behavior Expert
> Author – *I Can Read You Like a Book*

There is power in this book in Jim McCormick's keen insights about risk-taking and the practical tools he provides to help you take risks more successfully.

— BILL TREASURER
Author – *Right Risk* and *Courage Goes to Work*

I found *The Power of Risk* remarkable in how it showed me by example and definition how the many risks I took during my life and business career contributed to my success. I found the tremendously inspiring introduction alone to be worth the price of admission.

— IRA NEIMARK
Former CEO, Bergdorf Goodman
Author – *Crossing Fifth Avenue*

THE
POWER
OF RISK

Also by Jim McCormick:
365 Daily Doses of Courage

THE POWER OF RISK

How Intelligent Choices Will Make You More Successful

A STEP-BY-STEP GUIDE

Jim McCormick

Maxwell Press
San Francisco

The Power of Risk: How Intelligent Choices
Will Make You More Successful—A Step-by-Step Guide
by Jim McCormick

Copyright ©2008. All rights reserved.

Published by Maxwell Press, San Francisco, California

Printed in the United States of America

ISBN 978-0-9728520-0-5

TABLE OF CONTENTS

Dedication xi

Acknowledgments xiii

Introduction xv

CHAPTER ONE
YOUR RELATIONSHIP WITH RISK 1

CHAPTER TWO
YOUR NATURE 13

CHAPTER FIVE
YOUR PASSION AND CALLING 65

CHAPTER SIX
IDENTIFYING THE OPPORTUNITY 75

CHAPTER SEVEN
EVALUATING THE OPPORTUNITY 87

CHAPTER EIGHT
MAXIMIZING YOUR CHANCES OF SUCCESS 97

DEDICATION

To Mary Helen and Maryann, my risk-taking role models

ACKNOWLEDGMENTS

This book was a result of a maddeningly gradual process. Though in retrospect, it was not ready any sooner. I am not sure I would have ever written this book were it not for the example of my partner Maryann Karinch. While I was pursuing this project, she wrote no less than six books—all longer than this one—as only part of her professional pursuits. If she could create best-selling books like a human factory, certainly I could write at least one.

I would like to thank all those who provided persistent yet patient encouragement, particularly, my dear friends Robin Taylor and Dilenna Harris. Their faith in me meant more than they know. (I will now finally be able to deliver those ten copies Dilenna prepurchased years ago.)

For me, idea discovery is an interactive process. Along the way, I had the joy of having my thoughts challenged by some amazing men with extraordinary minds; Barry Sweet and James Barlow. Early on, I learned that following an unconventional path was acceptable and in some cases preferable from my volunteer parents, Ken and Wynona Brown.

To all the risk-takers, I say thank you. Whether they risk well or poorly, they were a source of insight. Our world is full of talented risk-takers who regularly show us the power of that most disquieting of concepts, risk.

There are also many who risk poorly and bring this potent tool into question. Yet at their expense, I gained insights.

One of the most thoughtful risk-takers I have encountered is a wonderful fellow you will meet in the eighth chapter. Brad Parsons not only moved to Maui to live a life of which most of us only dream, he also brilliantly displayed the power of intelligent risk-taking by expanding his horizons beyond the land.

I am deeply appreciative to the hundreds of people who included me in their profound life experience when they granted me the privilege of taking them for their first skydive. Their confidence in such a time of discovery and vulnerability is an honor beyond words. Being a part of such a transformative event never became routine. Their observations both before and after their jumps inspired much thought on the merits of taking risks.

The tandem skydiving student who most impressed me with his commitment and resilience was my father, Dean McCormick. Until he asked me to take him for his first skydive to celebrate his 73rd birthday, I did not realize that my risk-taking genes came from both parents.

Finally, I would like to acknowledge the brilliant musical philosopher Dan Fogelberg who in the dedication of his moving tribute to Native Americans, *The Spirit Trail,* uttered these indelible words that never left me and provided unending inspiration, *"To anyone who is traveling the path of heart as opposed to the path of convenience."* May we all.

INTRODUCTION

Our relationship with risk has a profound impact on the quality and character of our lives. If we are significantly risk *averse*, we will miss valuable opportunities. If we are significantly risk *inclined*, we may find ourselves regularly facing unproductive turmoil.

Most of us would benefit by taking a few more risks as long as we do it in an intelligent and thoughtful way. This stretching beyond our comfort zones often leads to significant and positive outcomes. Some of us would do well to either take fewer risks or take them in a more methodical way. This book can assist you regardless of where you fall on the risk-inclination spectrum.

Risk-taking is dear to me. I have consistently found that by challenging myself, I grow. My growth takes the form of new capabilities, fresh experiences, broader perspectives, and often increased confidence. I have observed that people who willingly risk challenging themselves enjoy increased vibrancy in their lives.

My own risk inclination manifests in many ways. The one I am best known for is skydiving. I have completed nearly 3,000 skydives over the course of 20 years and have earned five skydiving world records so far. Skydiving is an important part of my life.

I am not encouraging you to skydive nor am I promoting the sport. More broadly, I acknowledge that skydiving is a recreational activity like many others. But it differs from most in that skydiving forces you to confront some innate fears. Not many recreational activities confront you in the same way. This is a big part of the power of the skydiving experience.

Confronting any significant fear and proceeding in the face of it always has a powerful impact. It does not need to be as dramatic as skydiving or even involve a physical risk. Whenever we take action in spite of fear we grow. Taking action is empowering and liberates us. It bolsters our confidence. Observing this in both first-time and experienced skydivers has fueled my interest in the power of risk-taking as a means of personal development.

Skydiving provides insights into improving personal performance for additional reasons. Skydiving is not particularly physically demanding. Most of the work is done by the jump aircraft and gravity. But skydiving is mentally and emotionally demanding. For this reason, it is a valid life metaphor. Fortunately, most of us do not find our personal or professional success limited by physical abilities. But mental and emotional limitations affect us all. That's why learning to overcome the mental and emotional challenges of skydiving provides insights into how to do the same in other areas of our lives.

Finally, skydiving provides an impetus that is potentially profound. You have likely heard the encouragement to value each day knowing that it may be your last. You may have even heard people say they live their lives as though each day is their last. One reason to take risks is that we truly do not know how much time we have left. Opportunities missed today may never be presented again.

While it is good to value each day knowing it can never be repeated, the truth is we often take them for granted. But when I skydive, it forcefully reminds me of the fleeting nature of each passing day through what I call the Gift of Mortality. Strapping on a parachute and hurling myself out of a plane a few miles above the ground vividly reminds me that I will not be here forever.

While skydiving is not any riskier than many recreational activities—and statistically safer than some—it is somewhat unique because with each jump you are potentially ending your life. Unless you do the right things, your life will end. As a result, it provides an ever-present reminder that we are not here forever and we need to get on with our lives and aspirations. This is the Gift of Mortality.

You've likely been touched by the Gift of Mortality. It's presented to people when they are reminded—many times in profound terms—of the temporary nature of their lives. I've seen it in people who came close to losing their lives in accidents. The Gift of Mortality is also presented to people with terminal illnesses. When presented with the Gift of Mortality, some people welcome the reminder and change their lives in notable ways. They will often seize opportunities they would have previously let pass. They have an increased appreciation for life experiences, often take more risks, and have a greater sense of urgency.

Among my hopes for the people who read and utilize this book is that they embrace the Gift of Mortality even though they will hopefully live many more rich and purposeful years. At its core, the Gift of Mortality is a reminder to get on with it—whatever your life tasks may be.

Because thoughtful risk-taking is life-giving, because most of our barriers are self-imposed, and because we all have a limited time to make the impact we seek, I felt it important to create this book. I promise that if you take to heart the advice in this book and fully engage in the exercises it contains, you'll experience profound and wonderful changes in your life.

Life is meant to be an adventure. This book will help you make it so.

—Jim McCormick
Dominical, Costa Rica

ON-LINE TOOLS

Tools and forms that correspond to some of the exercises and assessments in this book are available at *www.TakeRisks.com/tools*. These tools may make it easier for you to complete the exercises and assessment. They will also be helpful should you choose to use these tools multiple times.

CHAPTER I

Your Relationship with Risk

Risk-taking is a celebration. Done well, it is the artful convergence of opportunity, talents, and resources. Taking risks is exciting. Done in a disciplined and intelligent manner, risk-taking is a powerful tool.

Yet we struggle with risk. Great tragedies are born of risk. But then so are stunning accomplishments. Risk can result in harm and death. It can also yield life-changing innovations.

How you regard risk is one of your defining characteristics and significantly influences most of your life choices.

The core question is this: Do you see risk as a threat to be minimized or a tool to be exploited?

The core question is this: Do you see risk as a threat to be minimized or a tool to be exploited? Is risk negative or positive?

Your level of risk inclination is yours and yours alone—*there is no wrong starting point.* You are unlikely to transition from an exceptionally cautious person into a cast-your-fate-to-the-wind risk-taker. But you can increase your ability to seize on risk as a tool that benefits you by using a measured and thoughtful approach to taking risks. The goal is to be a careful, disciplined and, as a result, successful risk-taker.

OPPORTUNITIES AWAIT

*"Few people get to do what they want
to do in life. Be one of them."*
ANDY BROER

Opportunities, large and small, abound. How you respond to these opportunities determines the life you lead. A willingness to take the risks that will seize these opportunities can expand your horizons, add excitement to your life, infuse it with vitality, bring new people into your world, and make life more fulfilling and enjoyable.

Following the process in this book will make you a more effective risk-taker and capable of taking advantage of opportunities. It will give you the insights and tools you need to be discerning, confident, and successful.

You may be satisfied with your life to this point, but looking to add more accomplishment, excitement, and joy. This book will help you do that.

Or you may not be at all pleased with what you've achieved to this point. If that's the case, this book can assist you greatly.

If you're less than pleased with your life so far, you have plenty of company. Research shows that half of adult Americans characterize their lives as only good, fair, or poor.[1] Clearly, you're not the only one who feels that way. But you can readily leave that state behind. This book will assist you in joining the other half of Americans who when asked said their lives are very good or even the best possible.

YOUR RISK QUOTIENT OR RQ

You are no doubt familiar with the concept of Intelligence Quotient or IQ—a test-derived score that attempts to measure intelligence. You may also be familiar with the concept of an Emotional Quotient or EQ—a measure of a person's emotional capacity to be effective and successful.

EQ makes sense as a concept. We all know that intelligence alone doesn't sufficiently indicate a person's talents. Emotional maturity and the ability to work effectively with others are also critical factors.

Each of us has a natural level of risk with which we feel comfortable. Call it your *Risk Quotient* or *RQ*. RQ is an indication of a person's risk inclination over a broad range of risk types. It is derived from a self-assessment you will go through in this chapter.

Until you actually have a chance to determine yours, think of your RQ as a number between 1 and 10—with 1 being very risk averse and 10 being very risk inclined—that indicates your general comfort with risk.

Risk Quotient is a concept that is used in investing and portfolio theory as an indication of an investor's risk tolerance. It also surfaces in assessing environmental issues, supply chain management, and the political stability of countries. It has not been previously applied as a personal development tool. Simply explained, risking less than your RQ makes you feel like you're not challenging yourself enough; risking beyond your RQ makes you feel uncomfortable.

> *"There is a precipice on either side of you—a precipice*
> *of caution and a precipice of over-daring."*
> WINSTON CHURCHILL

YOUR COMFORT ZONE

Your RQ is another way of looking at a familiar concept, your *Comfort Zone*. Most of the time, we function within our Comfort Zones where we feel reasonably at ease. Outside of it, things can quickly become frightening and your performance can become inconsistent.

When you think of your RQ as a point on a line between two extremes—between very risk averse and very risk inclined—your Comfort Zone includes everything to the left of your RQ as shown in the these graphics.

Your RQ

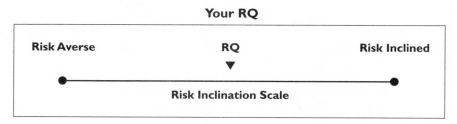

Your Comfort Zone

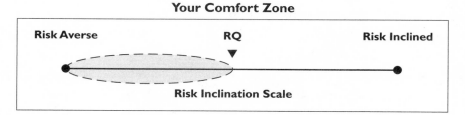

THE OUTCOME

This book provides tools that allow you to move your RQ to the right—that is, toward Risk Inclined and away from Risk Averse. In the process, you'll expand your Comfort Zone.

If you already have a high RQ, this book gives you tools to leverage your risk inclination and be successful more often.

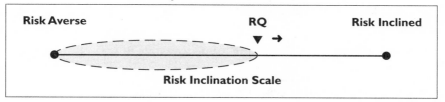

WHY INCREASE YOUR RQ?

Why make an effort to increase your RQ? Simple. Your response to opportunities determines the quality of your life. Shifting your RQ to the right means you'll feel comfortable taking more risks and thus taking advantage of more opportunities presented to you.

How much your RQ shifts is up to you. The size of the shift will be influenced by how committed you are to learning new skills, setting aside old behaviors, expanding your horizons, and exploiting opportunities. If you're like most, it will be an incremental process. Your RQ will move somewhat to the right. Once you have a few positive experiences and your confidence grows, your RQ will shift more to the right—toward being more Risk Inclined.

Your RQ is not static. It's always moving.

Your RQ is not static. It's always moving. You were not born with a certain RQ that can't change. Many things will influence your RQ. It can differ from day to day and week to week.

After a big success, you may feel more risk inclined; after a setback, you may or may not feel more risk averse. Research has shown that, in some cases, setbacks actually increase risk inclination.[2] Other influences can include recent changes or lack of them, financial security or lack of it, the state of your personal relationships, your level of satisfaction with your career and your life in general, your spiritual relationships, your age, and your level of confidence at a moment in time. These are just some of the influencers.

Nearly every aspect of your life influences your RQ.

The same traits that apply to individuals apply to organizations. Just as people have RQs, so do organizations. Similarly, the tools presented in this book can just as readily be used by organizations as individuals.

YOURS ALONE

"What you think of yourself is much more important than what others think of you."
SENECA

Try not to focus on how your RQ compares to others. It's not important and could distract you. While you can learn from observing what others do well and poorly in this realm, comparing yourself to them is simply not helpful. Your natural level of risk inclination—your RQ at this moment—results from a multitude of unique personal factors. It's influenced by the person you were at birth and all your life experiences since. Like you, it is unique.

While you can learn from observing what others do well and poorly in this realm, comparing yourself to them is simply not helpful.

Do not be concerned if your RQ is low (indicating a high degree of risk aversion). The goal is not to move your RQ all the way up to a 10 but rather to help you increase it somewhat so you can take intelligent risks that yield desired outcomes.

If you are naturally more comfortable with risk, that's great. As you've probably observed, you are uncommon. Still, this book will prove valuable to you. Using its tools will make more of the risks you take yield positive outcomes.

In addition, your ability to take risks successfully is likely stronger in some aspects of your life than others. As an example, you may be good at taking physical risks but lousy at taking career risks or emotional risks. This book will help you become better at seizing opportunities in more aspects of your life.

CREATING TURNING POINTS

Looking at past experiences can provide you with valuable insights. This first exercise helps you do just that. How much you get out of it will be determined by how much thought and effort you put into it.

Exercise—Your Turning Points

Step 1—Identifying Turning Points

On a fresh piece of paper, identify the *Turning Points* in your life. These are events that sent you off in a new direction—ones that changed your life, even a little bit, such as moving to a new school or meeting the person you married.

Some Turning Points will be more dramatic than others. Some will be positive and some negative. Some were your doing and some were imposed on you by circumstances or by others.

Start by looking for personal Turning Points in these areas:

- Location
- Education
- Relationships
- Occupation

Location—You may find Turning Points related to your geographic location. Take a look at the times you moved from one place to another.

Education—Your education will likely yield some Turning Points. These might include when you changed schools, took a break from school, returned to your studies, graduated, ended your formal education, decided to pursue graduate studies—anything along that line.

Relationships—More Turning Points will likely be associated with your relationships — friendships and dating relationships beginning and ending, marriage (beginning and perhaps ending), the birth of your children, their becoming independent, and the loss of loved ones are all points to consider.

Occupation—Your occupation is another place to look for Turning Points. Any promotions, demotions, and job changes—voluntary and forced—deserve particular attention.

These are only a few categories; a Turning Point is anything you consider important no matter what the category.

Examples of Turning Points

These examples of Turning Points may help you identify yours:

- Moving during your school years.
- Attending a summer camp or taking a trip.
- Losing a close friend or relative at a formative age.
- Running for a student government office.
- Going out for a high school or college sport.
- Attending college.
- Deciding not to attend college.
- Choosing your field of study.
- Relocating to take a promising job.
- Making a significant change in your career path.

- Pursuing an advanced degree.
- Getting married.
- Having children.
- Ending a marriage.
- Having a marriage ended against your wishes.
- Taking up a certain sport or activity.
- Getting laid off or fired from a job.
- Receiving a significant promotion.

Get the picture? Now it's your turn. Whether your Turning Points relate to location, education, relationships, occupation, or something else, start listing them.

Step 2—Your Self-Determined Turning Points

You'll likely find you have two types of Turning Points—the ones you *chose* and the ones *imposed* on you. The imposed Turning Points occurred due to circumstances beyond your control or the actions of others. They include things that happened as a child when you were not the decision-maker. For this exercise, don't focus on these; focus on the Turning Points that *you* chose. They're called Self-Determined Turning Points.

To set these Self-Determined Turning Points apart on your list, mark them in some way—highlight them, put a star by them, whatever works for you.

Continuing with the example, I marked each of the likely Self-Determined Turning Points with a star.

Examples of Self-Determined Turning Points
- Moving during your school years.
- Attending a summer camp or taking a trip.
- Losing a close friend or relative at a formative age.
- ☆ Running for a student government office.
- ☆ Going out for a high school or college sport.
- ☆ Attending college.

☆ •   Deciding not to attend college.

☆ •   Choosing your field of study.

☆ •   Relocating to take a promising job.

☆ •   Making a significant change in your career path.

☆ •   Pursuing an advanced degree.

☆ •   Getting married.

☆ •   Having children.

☆ •   Ending a marriage.

   •   Having your spouse decide to end your marriage.

☆ •   Taking up a certain sport or activity.

   •   Being laid off or fired from your job.

   •   Achieving a significant promotion.

Now, mark your own Self-Determined Turning Points in a similar way.

Step 3—Your Positive Self-Determined Turning Points

Considering only your Self-Determined Turning Points, the ones for which you were the decision maker, underline or circle the ones that had a positive outcome. These are the actions you're glad you took. Given the same circumstances, you may very well take them again.

Mark the Self-Determined Turning Points on your list that had a positive outcome.

Step 4—In Summary

On a new piece of paper, make three columns. Title the first one Turning Point. Title the second one Risks Taken. Leave the third column blank for now. We'll use it later.

In the first column, list only your Self-Determined Turning Points that had a positive outcome. In the example, they are the starred and underlined choices.

Positive Self-Determined Turning Points

Turning Point	Risks Taken	

Step 5—Risks Taken

In the second column corresponding to each Turning Point listed in the first column, list the risks you took that brought about that Turning Point. *Put some thought into this.* There are important insights here.

Hang on to this exercise. We will come back to it later and complete the third column.

Most, if not all, of your chosen Turning Points that resulted in a positive outcome required you to take some risk.

On-Line Tools

A Turning Points exercise that provides you with a consolidated version of the steps assessing past Turning Points as you are doing in this chapter and will continue in Chapter 4 is available at *www.TakeRisks.com/tools*.

The Point

Here is the point of this exercise so far. Most, if not all, of your chosen Turning Points that resulted in a positive outcome required you to take some risk. Remember, you had to venture out of your Comfort Zone to some extent. Significant positive Life Changes rarely occur without taking some risk.

This is how it works.

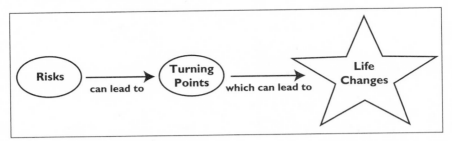

While this book will help you to take more constructive risks successfully, it could have an even greater impact than that. It could give you the tools and confidence you need to make decisions that lead to positive Turning Points. In turn, these can lead to positive and even profound Life Changes. By using the tools in this book, more of the risk you take will result in a positive outcome.

Let's put these tools to work.

CHAPTER 2

Your Nature

Your traits and talents make you unique. Countless experiences influence your ability to risk successfully and seize opportunities. This is your starting point. *There is no bad starting point.* Still, understanding your starting point is a critical first step in increasing your RQ.

THE TRUTH ABOUT RISK

> *"Growth means change and change involves risk,*
> *stepping from the known to the unknown."*
> GEORGE SHINN

Let's be honest. Almost nobody *likes* risk. Taking risks often frightens us and requires us to forgo control of the outcome. Because the results of taking some risks are bad, most of us see risk as something to avoid.

In contrast, when we were children, we took risks with abandon. We would try anything and had very limited judgment. This made us lousy risk-takers—we were happy to take risks but the outcomes were often bad. We were so curious and undeterred by risk that we weren't concerned about things like walking off the edge of a balcony or sticking our hand into that fascinating flame in the fireplace.

And what would happen when our natural desire to risk, explore, and discover took hold? Well, if it inspired us to do something that was a bad idea, we'd either experience its negative consequences firsthand or be greeted by a voice of authority. Taking an ill-advised risk as a child usually meant being redirected, disciplined, or even criticized by an authority figure—a parent, relative, teacher, sister, or brother.

Doing something fun—like responding to a burning desire to see how cool the mud in the back yard would look on our shirts—would often evoke a negative response. The same thing happened if we sprinted toward the street to greet a friend or retrieve a ball or if we stood too close to the edge of anything. "No!" "Be careful." "Don't do that," we'd hear.

And some kids never allowed their natural curiosity and risk inclination to be reigned in. How did our authority figures deal with them? Harshly. Those kids got an extra dose of discipline—something they certainly didn't want! How were these nonconformists characterized? As problems. As bad examples. "Now, you don't want to be like Ryan Smith," we'd hear. "That boy just doesn't listen," would come from the voice of authority.

So, what lesson did we learn? What message were we constantly receiving? *Risk is bad and something to be avoided.*

Please understand, I don't mean to suggest the authority figures who helped us survive childhood and adolescence had ill intent. Not at all. They did what probably needed to be done to temper our youthful enthusiasm and keep us safe due to our underdeveloped judgment. But it produced a powerful secondary outcome. Risk-taking became strongly associated with bad behavior and seen as negative.

Sadly, you may even recall a tragedy that touched you when a child or adolescent you knew got seriously injured or died due to a deadly combination of bad judgment, risk inclination, and fate. This kind of experience could have significantly affected your relationship with risk-taking, perhaps even without your realizing it.

OUR STRAINED RELATIONSHIP WITH RISK

"The only difference between a rut and
a grave is their dimensions."
ELLEN GLASGOW

This leads to a powerful dilemma. We've been socialized to avoid risk. The Comfort Zone is seductive. It is very tempting to just stay in it. We've seen or even experienced the negative results of youthful risk-taking gone awry.

We've been socialized to avoid risk.

Even more, it's common to prefer the known to the unknown. You may not be happy with certain aspects of your life, but at least you know what to expect. Sounds crazy, but you're probably saying to yourself, "Yup. Been there."

Here's an example of people preferring the known to the unknown, no matter how distasteful. Debra Jarvis is a cancer clinic chaplain at the Seattle Cancer Care Alliance. As a part of her role in supporting the caregivers in this organization, she has conducted training for nurses on dealing with the death that's an unavoidable part of their jobs.

Reverend Jarvis's training yielded an astounding discovery. Fully 80 percent—four out of five—of the 40 nurses who received the training said that, given a choice, they would prefer to die from cancer than any other cause. Only 20 percent said they would prefer to die in their sleep.[3] Isn't that amazing? These smart, well-educated healthcare professionals would rather experience the gradual, and commonly painful, ravages of cancer over simply expiring in their sleep.

It's hard to make sense of it, isn't it? But the appeal of the known over the unknown has power. So if you're not happy with certain aspects of your life yet you find the thought of change frightening, you're not alone. You're displaying a common tendency.

While we find change and risk frightening, we've also observed that risks sometimes bring about wonderfully positive outcomes. A joyous relationship probably started with someone taking a risk. The people we admire for their long-term accomplishments likely took many risks on the way to achieving their goals.

So how can you reconcile any ingrained risk aversion with a desire to seize opportunities and enjoy the rewards of successful risk-taking?

You can observe that "risk" and "comfort" have a tense relationship in your life. You would love the rewards that risk-taking brings. You may even enjoy the thrill of taking a risk. But stepping out of your Comfort Zone sets off all sorts of alarms—and may even evoke the admonitions of your childhood authority figures.

The goal is not to minimize risk. The goal is to minimize the possible negative outcomes of risk.

We all desire to remove unnecessary risk from our lives, but accepting *some* risk is vital to living a fulfilling life. The goal is not to minimize risk. The goal is to minimize the *possible negative outcomes* of risk. This is a central theme of this book. Risk-taking can be used to your advantage *and* increase your success and happiness.

What are you supposed to do? Exactly what you are doing, which is thoughtfully looking at the whole topic of taking intelligent risks successfully. By reading this book, you're putting time and energy into improving your ability to take risks well. And you're doing it with the benefit of the discernment and even the skepticism of an adult. You're on track!

NOT DUMB STUFF

*"Take calculated risks. That is quite
different from being rash."*
GENERAL GEORGE S. PATTON

Let's address an important issue—the need to avoid taking foolish, stupid, and gratuitous risks. I'm in no way encouraging you to do dumb stuff and take ill-advised risks. Exactly the opposite. What you'll learn as you work through the steps in this book will help you to be discerning in the risks you take. Most important, they will help you significantly increase the chances that the risks you take will have positive outcomes.

Avoid taking foolish, stupid, and gratuitous risks.

We all desire to avoid unnecessary risk—as we should. But the fact that you're reading this book suggests that you would like to take more risks to help you achieve your goals. Accepting some risk is a vital element of creating success and fulfillment.

YOUR STARTING POINT

The previous chapter introduced you to the concept of your personal Risk Quotient or your RQ. As this idea was presented, you probably assigned yourself an RQ somewhere between 1 and 10. You likely had a thought something like, "Oh, my RQ is about ..." Now you are going to determine your current RQ.

On the Risk Inclination Scale below, indicate your risk inclination with a mark anywhere on the line between Risk Averse and Risk Inclined.

To give you some reference points, numbers have been added to the scale, with 1 corresponding to Very Risk Averse and 10 being Very Risk Inclined. Be honest in identifying your current risk inclination. Wherever you place it is just fine. There are no wrong answers!

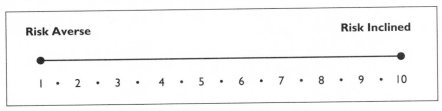

Your current risk inclination represents your perception of your current comfort level with risk. It hugely influences your perception of your risk-taking talents.

A BROADER LOOK

Now take a broader look at your current risk inclination. To start with, you want to move away from the idea of having a *single* level of risk inclination. Because such a general assessment is broad, it's likely not truly accurate. Why? Your risk inclination depends on the *type* of risk. As an example, how you respond to a financial risk can be much different than how you respond to an emotional risk.

Think about various types of risks—physical risks, career risks, financial risks, social risks, intellectual risks, creative risks, relationship risks, emotional risks, and spiritual risks. The next step is to indicate your risk inclination on the following topic-specific Risk Inclination Scales (on a scale of 1 to 10, with 1 being Very Risk Averse and 10 being Very Risk Inclined). Mark your personal risk inclination anywhere on the line between Risk Averse and Risk Inclined.

Physical Risks—Activities that involve some risk of injury. Riding a motorcycle, river rafting, rock climbing or skydiving are some examples.

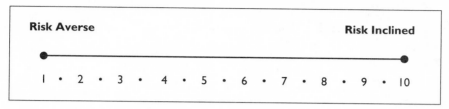

Career Risks—Risks such as pursuing job changes, taking on new responsibilities, or seeking promotions.

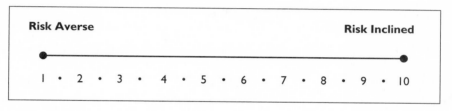

Financial Risks—Your risk tolerance in investing, borrowing, and lending money.

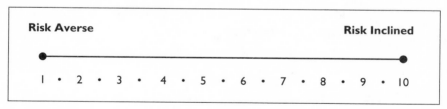

Social Risks—Risks like introducing yourself to someone you don't know, or putting yourself in an unfamiliar social situation even at the risk of possible embarrassment.

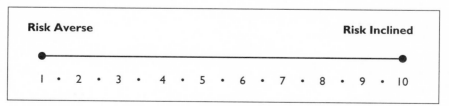

Intellectual Risks—Things like your willingness to study a difficult topic, pursue information that challenges your convictions, or read an intellectually challenging book.

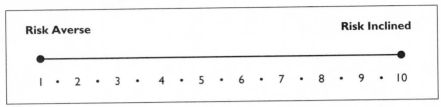

Creative Risks—Risks such as painting, drawing, taking on a writing challenge, or pursuing an unconventional design.

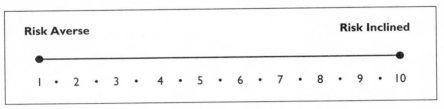

Relationship Risks—Risks such as a willingness to pursue a new relationship, spend time with someone despite an uncertain outcome, or make a relationship commitment.

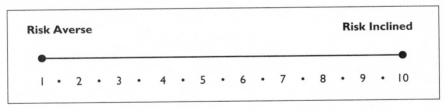

Emotional Risks—Willingness to allow yourself to be emotionally vulnerable.

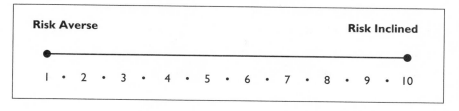

Spiritual Risks—Willingness to place your trust in concepts that may be improvable, or you do not fully understand.

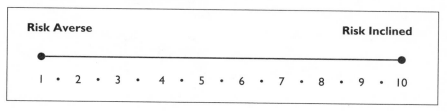

SO WHAT DOES THIS MEAN?

It's almost certain that the location of your risk inclination differs by the nature of the risk. You can draw three important insights from this realization.

- your risk inclination in one area does not define you
- we are all risk-takers
- you can learn from yourself

Your Risk Inclination in One Area Does Not Define You

Our comfort level with one type of risk often has too great an influence on our perception of our Overall Risk Inclination. Men in particular seem to allow their comfort level with physical risk inordinately influence their perception of their Overall Risk Inclination.

When I have shared my skydiving experiences in my presentation, many times audience members approach me after and say, "I could never do the kind of things you do. I'm not a risk-taker." But when time allows for a conversation, it always comes out that they're talented risk-takers in at least a few nonphysical aspects of their lives. They have characterized themselves inaccurately.

We Are All Risk-Takers

Everyone has the ability to take risks. The exception would be a timid, constrained person—and that person probably won't risk reading this book! The rest of us have the ability to take risks in some aspects of our lives.

Don't mislabel yourself. If you've been going through your life thinking, or even saying, "I'm not a risk-taker. I'm just not that courageous," I encourage you to drop that assessment. It may be that your risk inclination is highest when it comes to, for example, creative risks. That's good. It means you have aspects of your life in which you feel comfortable taking risks. *Do not undervalue this.* Wherever your higher risk inclination occurs, please know that lots of people would love to have your talent and ability.

You Can Learn from Yourself

From this self-assessment exercise you've learned that your risk inclination is stronger in some areas than others. The value in this awareness is being able to assess how you respond to opportunities that fall into these areas, then use these insights to assist you in bolstering your risk inclination in other areas.

So ask yourself, "Why am I more comfortable taking a certain type of risk?" "What do I do in those situations that would be helpful in other situations?" "Why am I more confident taking one type of risk than another—and how can I transfer that confidence elsewhere?" If you're willing to ask these questions, you will be rewarded with valuable insights.

This exercise has given me valuable insights. For one, I've observed that I'm more risk inclined when I believe I am in a position to significantly influence the outcome of the risk. I get this by observing my comfort level with some physical risks and not others.

With skydiving, for example, I know that my training, currency, preparation, and execution significantly influence my safety. As such, as long as I pay attention to all of these elements, it's an acceptable risk for me. But I've never been comfortable with riding a motorcycle because it seems that my safety is enormously influenced by the people driving cars and trucks. I'm not comfortable trusting my own safety to drivers who may be distracted or are just plain unaware.

I've affirmed this insight further in that I have a hard time taking relationship risks. My past experience has shown me that, while I can *influence* the outcomes of relationships, I cannot and should not try to *control* their outcome. That makes it hard for me to take those risks.

Looking closely at your risk-taking self-assessments above can give you similar insights.

YOUR STARTING POINT, REVISITED

Now that you have broadened your perspective of your risk inclination, this is a good time to reassess your Overall Risk Inclination. Go back and look at what you indicated as your risk inclination for the nine topic-specific Risk Inclination Scales. With these assessments in mind, revisit the position of your current Overall Risk Inclination and mark it below.

OVERALL RISK INCLINATION

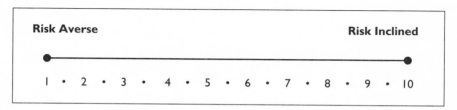

If your current risk inclination is different than it was earlier, pay attention. You now have a better assessment of where you see yourself. If your

Overall Risk Inclination is in the same place as it was before, that means this process has helped you confirm your initial assessment.

DETERMINING YOUR RQ

I've administered this risk profile to thousands of people. I'm always intrigued to see that some people show their Overall Risk Inclination as being significantly different than the risk profile they've indicated in the nine specific risk types. Most often when this occurs, people mark their Overall Risk Inclination much lower than their topic-specific risk tolerances would suggest.

This variance led me to develop the concept of the personal Risk Quotient (RQ). Your RQ is simply the average of the values you indicated for the nine specific risk types. For example, if the numerical value of all your risk inclinations was 6, then your RQ is 6. If half were 4 and half were 7, then your RQ is 5.5.

To determine your RQ, go back and total the numerical value of the risk inclination you indicated for the nine topic-specific risk types and divide that total by 9. That is your current RQ.

The RQ is a more accurate and genuine assessment than the self-assessment of Overall Risk Inclination because it is derived from the nine more specific assessments. It also eliminates the problem of people who perceive their revised Overall Risk Inclination as being out of alignment with their risk inclination in the nine topic-specific risk areas.

I've been using a risk profile assessment consisting of these questions for a number of years as part of my presentations. In those situations, the people who complete the assessment keep the assessment for future reference and to assure confidentiality. While I ask them to indicate any change between the first and last question, that's not a scientific way of determining norms and patterns. So while writing this book, I had the survey administered to over 300 people, in person and on-line. The results are detailed at the end of this chapter. Many interesting insights can be gleaned from this research.

Most likely, your RQ and your second assessment of your Overall Risk Inclination are similar. For about half of the people surveyed, it was effectively the same. Only a small percentage of people had RQs significantly higher or lower than their revised Overall Risk Inclination.

On-Line Tools

A Personal Risk Profile that provides you with a consolidated version of the self-assessment you have gone through in this chapter is available at *www.TakeRisks.com/tools*. It may be an easier way for you to take this self-assessment again in the future and share it with others.

WHAT'S NORMAL?

Understandably, you may be wondering what's normal—that is, where most people rank their risk inclination. To start with, don't be too concerned about "normal." Your goal is to have a level of risk inclination that serves you best. How yours compares to others is not all that important. Yet, it's reasonable to want a sense of where you stand compared to others. If this is a question you would like to answer, you will want to look at the detailed review of the results of this research in the Appendix near the end of this book.

ANOTHER REFERENCE POINT

A sense of where your risk inclination falls in relationship to others can be gained from your response to the following scenario.

Your Situation—Assume you're the only income earner in your family and you have a secure job that will continue to provide you with income for as long as you choose to work.

The Opportunity—Assume you're offered an equally secure job that will also provide you with income for as long as you choose to work. Your income will be one of the following with equal chances of either occurring. Either—

- Double your current income, or
- Two-thirds of your current income.

These are the only two options and the chances of either occurring are the same—50 percent.

The Question—Would you take the new job or keep your current job?

How Others Responded—If you said you'd take the new job, you're in the minority, which suggests you are more comfortable taking that kind of risk than most. If you said no to the opportunity, you have lots of company. Over 11,000 adults were asked this question and more that 75 percent said they would decline the new job.[4] How you responded to this gives you a sense of where you stand in relationship to others.

Now for a second question.

Your Situation—Again, assume you're the only income earner in your family and you have a secure job that will continue to provide you with income for as long as you choose to work.

The Opportunity—And again, assume you're offered an equally secure job that will also provide you with income for as long as you choose to work. This time the best case remains the same: there is a 50 percent chance your income will double. The worst case is slightly different and not as bad. Instead of there being a 50 percent chance your income could decrease by 33 percent, the worst case is that your income drops by 20 percent.

This means your income will be one of the following with equal chances of either occurring. Either—

- Twice your current income, or
- 80 percent of your current income.

The Question—The question is the same as before. Would you take the new job or keep your current job?

How Others Responded—Again, if you said you would take the new job, you're still in the minority. About two-thirds of the same people who were asked first question said they would decline this opportunity.[5] If you said no to the opportunity, you continue to have lots of company.

To review, only about 25 percent of those asked said they would take the first opportunity and about 33 percent said they would take the second one. The responses to these questions did not differ significantly based on gender.

If you said you would take either or both of the opportunities, you're more comfortable taking that kind of risk than most—at least when it comes to career risks. If you said you would decline both opportunities, you have similar feelings about career risks as most people.

Don't be too concerned about how your current level of risk inclination compares to others.

Again, I encourage you not to be too concerned about how your current level of risk inclination compares to others. With that said, you now have a good idea of how you compare to most.

All of this leads you to a better understanding of your personal risk inclination as expressed by your Risk Quotient. Keep in mind, what you have identified is your RQ at this point in time. It is not static, so be open to it changing.

> *"Take stock of your fears now and see how many of them are senseless. If you are honest with yourself you will probably find most of them are groundless."*
> **DALE CARNEGIE**

CHAPTER 3

Your Talents and Gifts

*Few things are sadder than watching a person
passionately pursue a course for which they are
ill suited—particularly when that same passion,
when applied toward a course that aligns with
their talents, would yield them so much more.*
JIM MCCORMICK

Improving your ability to risk successfully requires you to
have a clear understanding of your innate talents—your
Natural Skill Set. This sounds obvious. But very few people take time to sit
down and inventory their strengths and weaknesses.

Think of it like this—if you were to set out in your car on a 2,500 mile
trip without a map, you may reach your destination eventually, but you'd
probably make a number of wrong turns and do some backtracking. You

may arrive at your intended destination, but you'll almost certainly waste time and energy getting there.

The same is true when it comes to understanding your Natural Skill Set. Having a clear understanding will help you—

- Be more effective,
- Reduce frustrations and negative outcomes,
- Establish better goals,
- Increase your chances of realizing those goals,
- Achieve your goals sooner and with less effort,
- Better select which opportunities to seize, and
- Make you more successful at taking risks.

Clearly, having an accurate sense of your Natural Skill Set is tremendously valuable. So your next step is to discern your Natural Skill Set.

NATURAL SKILL SET

> *"God has given each of us the ability*
> *to do certain things well."*
> THE APOSTLE PAUL

Your Natural Skill Set consists of the things at which you excel, the things you're reasonably good at, and the things you don't do well at all. All of these are a part of your Natural Skill Set.

Your Natural Skill Set consists of the things at which you excel, the things you're reasonably good at, and the things you don't do well at all.

Exercise—Your Natural Skill Set

Take a blank piece of paper, lined or unlined, and create three columns. Title the left column "Strengths," the middle column "Serviceable Skills," and the right column either "Weaknesses" or "Areas for Improvement," whichever you prefer.

Natural Skill Set

Strengths	Serviceable Skills	Weaknesses or Areas for Improvement

Where your capabilities fall depends on both your ability and how much fulfillment you get from a certain type of task. Simply stated, it is a matter of how good you are and how much you enjoy it.

Category	Capability	Fulfillment
Strengths	high	high
Serviceable Skills	high	low
Weaknesses or Areas for Improvement	low	low

Now, start filling in your columns. Your initial entries will probably come easily. Go with them. List whatever comes to mind.

Strengths

Under Strengths, list the capabilities that come to you naturally. These are the things you do with seemingly no effort. You can do them without a lot of thought.

As an example, you may have an excellent sense of direction that makes you excel at navigating. Do others often hand you the map and ask you to find the best route?

Or you may be a good negotiator. Have you ever had friends ask you to haggle with a street merchant or negotiate a car purchase for them because "you're really good a getting a better price"?

You may have innate artistic talents. Do your colleagues compliment you on the drawings and sketches you create during a boring meeting?

Among your strengths may be math, or singing, or conversation, or memory, or cooking. Whatever they are, list them all. They don't need to be career related. Think broadly in all areas of your life.

Realize that you have always been good at these things that come with ease. They are probably, but not always, activities you enjoy—ones that make others say "you make that look so easy" or "you're a natural."

Skills and Passions Travel

My friend Blythe unintentionally illustrated one of her natural skills— and passions—on her vacation.

Blythe owns a pet care business. Her company takes care of people's pets when they are away. A while back, she joined a girlfriend for two carefree weeks in Tahiti. When she returned, she told me that after only a few days on the island, she noticed a lot of poorly fed dogs and cats. For the rest of her vacation, she spent a few hours each day taking waste food from the resort's kitchen around to the animals on the island.

Is Blythe in the right profession? I don't think there is any question. There she was, 4,000 miles from home, spending her vacation doing what she would be doing if she was home working—caring for animals. Clearly, Blythe has aligned her skills and passions with her work.

Does this story bring to mind any of your skills and passions?

**We are inclined to undervalue the talents
and abilities that come to us easily.**

Undervaluing Strengths

Here is an important note. We are inclined to undervalue the talents and abilities that come to us easily. When something comes to us readily and requires little effort, it is easy to value it less than abilities we had to work hard to acquire. Watch for this. If a strength comes to mind and your immediate thought is "oh, that's no big deal," you've found an ability you undervalue.

**To identify your strengths, ask friends,
family members, and colleagues this
question: "What am I really good at?"**

Insights from Others

If you've put all the strengths that come to mind on your list—or you're stumped—solicit input from others. To identify your strengths, ask friends, family members, and colleagues this question: "What am I really good at?" Ask them which specific abilities they consider to be your strengths. Listen carefully and you'll gain valuable insights.

Serviceable Skills

Serviceable Skills are things you do reasonably well when you have to, but require more effort than those on your Strengths list. You don't find doing these things easy, but if you have to, you can pull them off.

An example for me is accounting. I have done well in the few accounting courses I've taken. I'm good at the order, sequence, and logic of accounting, but I hate doing it. If I had to do accounting all day, I'd be wandering the streets shouting through a bullhorn declaring the end of the world. That tells me that accounting belongs on my Serviceable Skills list. I can do it but definitely prefer not to.

What can you do, perhaps even do well, but prefer not to? This is what goes in your Serviceable Skills column.

Weaknesses or Areas for Improvement

These activities cause you to struggle and can even make you cringe. You'd rather have a tooth pulled without anesthesia than do some of them. Or you may not find them distasteful, but you just don't do them well.

I offered you a choice of how to title this column between "Weaknesses" or "Areas for Improvement." This is because there may be some things in this column you want to improve while there may be others you have no interest in working on.

Again, input from others will be helpful here. Ask friends, family members, and colleagues what you are *not* good at to gain valuable insights. Plus, they may enjoy telling you!

Additional Insights

You can do more than this to get a full sense of your Natural Skill Set. If you have the desire and resources, you can invest in all sorts of career and personality testing. You can find professionals and organizations, as well as resources on the Internet, that will help you better understand your Natural Skill Set.

If you choose to invest in these types of services, I suggest working with well-trained professionals to help you interpret the results of whatever assessment instruments you complete. Professional interpretation is vital to furthering your understanding. Doing this may cost more, but I recommend it because self-administered tests are always susceptible to misinterpretation. This information is too important to run that risk!

Having gained these insights, your next question is "what do I do with this information?"

EXPLOIT YOUR STRENGTHS

Be mindful of your strengths when selecting the risks you take and opportunities you pursue. This seems self-evident, but it's amazing how often people pursue opportunities that are at odds with their Natural Skill Set.

For example, if your strengths include persistence, goal orientation, and good people skills, you're probably well-suited for a sales role. If these are not among your strengths, you may not be suited for sales.

If you are a big-picture thinker who can easily comprehend a complex concept and all its implications, you have a great talent. However, you may not be great at keeping track of details. If so, you're not likely to be good in an administrative support role or an activity like bookkeeping. But you can excel in the role of the visionary as long as you have others to handle the details and implementation.

> **The more you select opportunities, risks, and goals that are consistent with your Natural Skill Set, the more successful you will be.**

This concept is obvious: The more you select opportunities, risks, and goals that are consistent with your Natural Skill Set, the more successful you will be.

> *"If you have been given gifts, they are there for you to return the gift in some measure. I would feel very badly about having a gift and just ignoring it."*
> PETER USTINOV

BOLSTER YOUR WEAKNESSES

Your Natural Skill Set exercise has given you a list of all the things you're not that good at. "Great," you might be thinking, "but what good is that?" It's valuable because you now have a strategy for exploiting this information. Your strategy is to:

1. Be Selective
2. Improve your Talents
3. Pursue a Maximum Return on Effort
4. Acknowledge Immovable Limitations
5. Call on Others

> *"Difficulties are meant to rouse, not discourage."*
> WILLIAM ELLERY CHANNING

BE SELECTIVE

Just as you want to gravitate toward opportunities and constructive risks that use your strengths, you want to shy away from those that require talents in areas where you come up short. When contemplating an opportunity, ask, "How well does my Natural Skill Set suit me to the tasks that will be required to succeed?"

Realize that there may be opportunities, roles, and jobs that appeal to you but don't align well with your Natural Skill Set. Approach them cautiously.

When contemplating an opportunity, you need to ask yourself, "How well does my Natural Skill Set suit me to the tasks that will be required to succeed?"

Let me give you an example. My friend is a talented graphic designer and well established in her community. Many of her clients were telling her that the local printer was having persistent quality and delivery problems.

Because they felt frustrated, they were seeking other printers. My friend thought this may be a good opportunity to expand her services and increase her revenue by opening a print shop.

We sat down and talked. On a blank pad of paper, we worked together to describe her Natural Skill Set, just as I have encouraged you to do. On a separate piece of paper, we listed the talents required to run a successful printing operation. We then put the two sheets of paper side by side.

What did we find? There was not a good match. My friend is artistic and creative but not good at administrative tasks. Her Natural Skill Set suits her well as a designer, but probably not as a print shop owner. She decided to go in a different direction that aligned with her Natural Skill Set. She learned to assist her frustrated clients, but in a different way.

"Twenty years from now you will be more disappointed by the things that you didn't do than by the ones you did do. So throw off the bowlines. Sail away from the safe harbor. Catch the trade winds in your sails. Explore. Dream. Discover."
MARK TWAIN

IMPROVE YOUR TALENTS

You don't have to avoid opportunities that require skills that aren't your strengths. You can take steps to bolster your talents. For example, you may be able to move some of your Serviceable Skills into (or at least closer to) your Strengths column. The same with Weaknesses or Areas for Improvement. With effort and commitment, you may be able to move something from that column to the Serviceable Skills column.

If you identify skills you need to improve and are ready to commit the time and energy to make that happen, I applaud you. But before you charge forward, I encourage you consider these two concepts: Return on Effort and Immovable Limitations.

*"Flying is about learning your limitations
and staying within them — but constantly
expanding your limitations."*
GENERAL JIMMY DOOLITTLE

PURSUE A MAXIMUM RETURN ON EFFORT

Presumably, you'll be able to improve the skill you choose to bolster. But before you get started, ask this question: "Would I be better served to put the same time and effort toward something I am already good at?"

The answer may be "no." You may have identified an element of your Natural Skill Set that really needs to be improved for you to get where you want to go.

But the answer to the same question may be "yes." You may conclude you would do much better to accept your lesser talent level in one area and instead work to get the maximum results out of your innate strengths.

**Before deciding to bolster a skill,
consider your best Return on Effort.**

Let's look at an example of someone who had to decide where she could get the best Return on Effort.

Samantha the Sales Maven

Samantha—her friends call her Sam—has been in sales for a few years. She's good at it. The Strengths in her Natural Skill Set include people skills, persistence, and being goal oriented. Due to Samantha's success, her employer keeps rewarding her with larger accounts.

These larger accounts present Samantha with a challenge. The decision makers for these new larger accounts are often more sophisticated than they were at the smaller accounts where Samantha started. In particular, Samantha is finding she needs to better understand accounting and finance to deal with these more sophisticated customers.

This is a problem. Samantha has always struggled with accounting and finance. She's simply not good at it. She barely made it though the accounting classes she had to take in the past and only because she got a lot of help from her friends.

Samantha thought she had put accounting classes behind her forever, which is exactly her preference. But now accounting has reared its ugly head. Samantha realizes she will be much less successful if she doesn't bolster her understanding of the financial analysis that influences her customer's buying decisions.

Here's the Return on Effort decision Samantha faced. Does she enroll in an Accounting for Sales Professionals class at the local community college, knowing it will be a real struggle and provides no certainty it will improve her abilities? Or does Samantha put the same time and effort toward an activity that comes naturally? What would that activity be?

Samantha had recently joined two industry associations. Many of her current and prospective customers belong to these associations. She knows they are a great way to build relationships with decision makers in her target market. One of these associations loves Samantha's energy and has offered her a leadership role that will raise her profile in the industry and give her more access to customers and prospects.

Due to limited time, Samantha can't do both the accounting class and the industry association leadership role. This is the core of Samantha's Return on Effort decision.

Now from this description, we don't have enough information to advise Samantha on her decision. And that's not the point of this illustration. The point is to describe a real-life situation to help you recognize a Return on Effort decision when it confronts you.

ACKNOWLEDGE IMMOVABLE LIMITATIONS

Somewhere in your childhood, you may have received loving encouragement from adults who told you that "you can do anything you set your mind to." Bless them. They may well have been right. And even if they weren't, the "you can do anything you set your mind to" approach to life is a great way to live. Now comes the big qualifier.

> **You may be able to set your mind to something your Natural Skill Set does not naturally lead you to, put forth massive effort over many years and possibly achieve it. But the same effort over the same amount of time directed toward something that is consistent with your Natural Skill Set will yield far greater results.**

While you may ultimately be able to achieve anything you pursue with passion and persistence, *you are clearly better suited for some things than others.*

Yes, you may be able to set your mind to something your Natural Skill Set doesn't naturally lead you to, put forth massive effort over many years and possibly achieve it. But the same effort over the same amount of time directed toward something that is consistent with your Natural Skill Set will yield far greater results.

Think of it this way: Attempting to take a risk and seize an opportunity that doesn't align well with your Natural Skill Set is like using an old, cheap bicycle in competitive cycling. Yes, you can work extra hard and possibly be competitive. But when you choose an opportunity that aligns with your Natural Skill Set, it's like having a state-of-the-art, multi-thousand-dollar bike. The same effort you put in will result in much greater success.

Let's take an example of a fellow who isn't exceptionally tall or athletically gifted. As a result, his Natural Skill Set doesn't lead him to be a professional basketball player. Fortunately, this fellow never decided his life goal was to play in the National Basketball Association. Had he adopted that goal, he would have been destined to a life of frustration.

However, if he did have an undying passion for basketball, he could still leverage that passion despite not having the physical gifts to be a player. He could pursue a role in announcing, officiating, promotions, coaching, sports training, management, or several other roles related to the sport.

**Can you do anything you set your mind to?
Within reason, yes. Should you attempt to? No.**

Can you do anything you set your mind to? Within reason, yes. Should you attempt to? No. Please understand. I'm not trying to discourage you. Absolutely not. I want you to achieve as much success, joy, and fulfillment as possible. My point is this: When you choose the opportunities you pursue wisely and are ever mindful of your natural strengths and weaknesses, you will enjoy much more success and satisfaction.

CALL ON OTHERS

The final element of your strategy for exploiting your Natural Skill Set is to call on others. Know when to turn over certain tasks to others. There are things on your Weaknesses or Areas for Improvement list that you'd be well served to have someone else handle for you.

Know when to turn over certain tasks to others.

I know where some of mine are. My dislike of detail and precision means I've had to find others to handle tasks such as bookkeeping. Even with all the great bookkeeping software available, I still can't stomach bookkeeping. When I tried doing it myself, it just never got done.

Creating and maintaining my websites is another example. I may be able to develop Serviceable Skills in this area, but my Return on Effort, compared to what I can achieve pursuing other tasks, would be negligible. The same is true for editing books and articles, other tasks that don't align well with my Natural Skill Set.

In my career, I've observed that the people who ascend to the top of their organizations have a keen awareness of their deficiencies. They probably wouldn't have done so well in their careers without this awareness. What do they do with these insights? They call on others to assist them in their weak areas.

> **The people who ascend to the top of their organizations have a keen awareness of their deficiencies.**

You might be thinking "but I don't run a large organization and I don't have a staff to delegate things to." I have two comments for you. First, there's almost always a way to get assistance from others who have strengths that correspond to your weaknesses. Pursue it. Second, you will have times when you're forced to do things you aren't well suited to. That's reality. Do them reluctantly, don't make a habit of doing them, and delegate them as soon as you can.

A MOVING TARGET

The skills and talents that have gotten you to this point in your life may not be the same ones that will serve you well going forward. As you move through life, you'll likely find that the methods that worked earlier no longer work as well.

An example would be the construction worker who, in his 20s, used his physical strength to accomplish tasks. That same fellow, in his 50s, will find his strength fading. Therefore, he'd need to rely more on cleverness to get the same results he could achieve in the past using shear strength. Generally speaking, what we accomplish with strength early in our lives needs to be approached more with finesse and less with strength as we age.

Another example is the attractive young woman who came to rely on her youthful good looks while in her 20s to garner attention and make an impression. A few decades hence, with her youthful appearance gone, she may need to rely instead on her intellect, charm, and the wisdom gained from life experiences to achieve the same results.

The idea that the skills we need change as we proceed through life is as old as the ages. Sophocles expressed the concept in the play *Oedipus the King* that he wrote around 440 B.C. The play includes the Riddle of the Sphinx, which asks, "What has one voice and is four-footed, two-footed and three-footed?" The answer is "man." We crawl on all fours as babies, walk upright in the prime of our lives, and often need a cane in old age. This ancient wisdom shared by Oedipus applies as well today as it did almost 2,500 years ago.

> **The skills that have served you well in the past may not be the same ones that will continue to serve you well in the future.**

My advice is to remain agile over time. The skills that have served you well in the past may not be the same ones that will continue to serve you in the future. Keep this in mind as you focus on which skills to bolster.

THE STRENGTH/WEAKNESS PARADOX

Now that you have a good understanding of your Natural Skill Set, you have a valuable tool that will make you more successful at taking risks. But there is an important insight you need to keep in mind as you seek to exploit your natural strengths.

> *Our greatest strengths and weaknesses are*
> *one in the same. All your strengths have*
> *the potential to become weaknesses.*
> **JIM MCCORMICK**

Any positive trait, if applied in the extreme, can become negative. Even if this idea has occurred to you before, it deserves additional discussion because it is so powerful. Let me give you some examples.

Any positive trait, if applied in the extreme, can become negative.

Have you ever come across people who are impressively goal oriented? Once they lock onto a goal, they almost certainly achieve it. The goal occupies a prominent place in their lives and becomes a significant part of who they are.

To a point, this strength serves them well. But it can become negative. Goal orientation taken to the extreme can become so intense that they lose their "peripheral vision"— that is, their ability to be aware of their setting and new opportunities. They even risk becoming narrow-minded. As a result, a valuable strength turns into a limiting weakness.

Here is another example. Think of people who are wonderfully thoughtful and caring—the kind who simply can't do enough for others. They seem to have a genetic predisposition to be kind and helpful. This wonderful trait can turn negative when they do not know when to back off, especially if they become intrusive and meddling. Again, a strength has become a weakness.

Any strength can become a negative. This is the Strength/Weakness Paradox.

Get the picture?
- Precision can turn into perfectionism or even intolerance.
- A person with a gregarious nature can become unproductive or tedious.
- A person with strong analytical skills can have tunnel vision.

- A discerning and observant person can become judgmental and alienating.
- A person who is passionate and enthusiastic can become overbearing.
- A person who is careful can become overly cautious and miss opportunities.
- A confident person can become overconfident and make poor decisions.
- An intense individual can become unaware of others and their surroundings.
- A broadminded person can become unfocused and cast about aimlessly.
- A person who has high personal standards can fall victim to perfectionism.
- A goal-oriented person can become so focused as to lose perspective and lapse into tunnel vision.
- A person who is thoughtful and caring can become intrusive and meddling.

On and on it goes. Any strength can become a negative. This is the Strength/Weakness Paradox.

"Have patience with all things,
but mostly with yourself."
ST. FRANCIS deSALES

Keeping this information in mind, now go back to the page where you listed the Strengths in your Natural Skill Set. Look at each strength you have listed and consider how, if a strength is allowed to become extreme, it can turn into a negative trait. Carefully absorb these insights. They can help you be more discerning as you seize opportunities in your life.

On-Line Tools

A Strength/Weakness Paradox exercise that builds on this concept and allows you to quickly assess the positive and negative manifestations of your three primary talents is available at *www.TakeRisks.com/tools*.

CHAPTER 4

Tapping Into Your Courage and Passion

"To be what we are and to become what we are
capable of becoming, is the only end in life."
ROBERT LOUIS STEVENSON

What have you accomplished so far in this book? Let's review.

- You've started to think about where your Risk Quotient falls on the Risk Inclination Scale, both generally and for specific types of risks.
- You've been reminded that it doesn't help to compare your RQ to others and that yours is as unique as you are.
- You've realized—or been reminded—that your risk tolerances are higher in some aspects of your life than in others.

- You've gained insights into why your risk inclination is higher in some areas than others.
- You've identified the positive Turning Points that have occurred so far in your life and the risks you took to bring them about.
- You've thought about how your risk inclination has been influenced by your socialization as a child and adolescent.
- You've described your Natural Skill Set and learned how to exploit and bolster it for your benefit.
- You've contemplated the possibility that your greatest strengths can, at times, become your greatest weaknesses.

You've made a good start in establishing a baseline, an understanding, of your nature and talents. The next step is to build on these understandings. In this chapter, you'll learn how to further leverage the insights you've gained to make you more effective at taking risks successfully.

THE RISK AVOIDANCE OPTION

> *"What kind of man would live where there is no daring?*
> *I don't believe in taking foolish chances, but nothing*
> *can be accomplished without taking any chance at all."*
> CHARLES LINDBERGH

It's time for a mindset check. I've said it before, but I want to be very direct: Pursuing opportunities requires you to take risks. Risk brings with it all sorts of negative connotations. In most people's minds, as we have discussed, risk is regarded as something to be avoided.

Pursuing opportunities requires you to take risks.

In later chapters, we'll get specific about minimizing the risks involved in pursuing opportunities. Then we'll work on maximizing the chances that any risks you take will result in positive outcomes. But at the end of the day, we can't escape the fact that taking some risk is part of the process. This may require a mindset shift.

THE MINDSET SHIFT

As noted earlier, the goal is not to minimize risk but to minimize *possible negative outcomes* of risk and embrace risk-taking as a powerful tool.

Here's this idea expressed graphically.

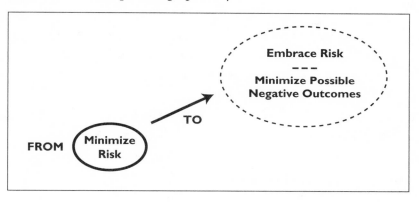

The goal is not to minimize risk but to minimize *possible negative outcomes* of risk and embrace risk-taking as a powerful tool.

If you are predisposed to want to avoid risk, give yourself a powerful gift. Move to the mindset of *embracing risk and minimizing possible negative outcomes*. This is a critical distinction.

A risk-free life does not exist. Pursuing one will just frustrate you and wring joy, excitement, and accomplishment out of your life.

Think about the implications of trying to purge your life of risk. To start with, you will not succeed. A risk-free life does not exist. Pursuing one will just frustrate you and wring joy, excitement, and accomplishment out of your life.

An impassioned effort to remove risk from your life will not only fail, but will divert your energy and put you into a persistently negative mindset. You will be fighting a losing battle. In addition, attempting to insulate yourself from risk will deprive you of the rewards that come from intelligent risk-taking.

An impassioned effort to remove risk from your life will not only fail, but will divert your energy and put you into a persistently negative mindset.

A reality check is needed here. Face facts: We don't have nearly as much control over events as we'd like to think we have. A great part of our lives is beyond our control. In fact, trying to control every aspect of our lives is a fool's mission destined to failure. The far superior alternative is to accept this reality. From there, we can put the "I want to control everything" energy toward more positive uses.

Comedian Gilda Radner's wonderful quote speaks volumes about this:

> *"Life is about not knowing, having to change,*
> *taking the moment and making the best of it,*
> *without knowing what's going to happen next.*
> *Delicious ambiguity."*
> GILDA RADNER

Wouldn't it be nice if we could reclaim all the energy we've expended in the past trying to control uncontrollable outcomes? But while we can't change the past, we can do everything possible to make that inclination a part of the past and not the present or the future.

Wouldn't it be nice if we could reclaim all the energy we've expended in the past trying to control uncontrollable outcomes?

APPLAUD YOURSELF

By just reading this book, you're setting yourself apart. After all, revising your relationship with risk is never easy. As you work toward building this new relationship, take credit for your efforts.

Revising your relationship with risk is never easy.

When asked to rank the values they hold most dear, thousands of Americans ranked a "sense of accomplishment" seventh of eighteen. Ranked first was "family security" followed by values such as "freedom, self-respect, and happiness."[6] Carefully following the steps in this book will provide you with results that will bolster your own sense of accomplishment.

Another likely outcome of applying the methods provided in this book is a bit more excitement in your life. Where did an exciting life fall among the eighteen values people ranked as most important to them? Seventeenth.[7] That helps explain why so many people lead rather lackluster lives. If a desire for excitement is near the bottom of their list of concerns, living less-than-thrilling lives is pretty much inevitable.

LIBERATING YOURSELF FROM RISK AVOIDANCE CONDITIONING

"Fears are educated into us, and can,
if we wish, be educated out."
KARL A. MENNINGER, PH.D.

Chapter 2 addressed how we were socialized early in our lives to avoid risk. This was done by authority figures—in most cases with the best of intentions to help us survive childhood and adolescence. In many ways, this socialization led to our seeing risk as negative.

In those early years, our innate comfort with risk was not balanced with judgment. This imbalance could—and at times probably did—lead to negative outcomes. We clearly needed the redirection and guidance authority figures provided us.

> **Through maturity and life experiences, you've acquired judgment you did not have as a child and youth, but you probably haven't consciously readjusted your attitude toward risk.**

But look at what's happened since. Through maturity and life experiences, you've acquired judgment you didn't have as a child and youth, but you probably haven't consciously readjusted your attitude toward risk. It may still be too influenced by negative associations from your early years when you had much more limited judgment. That leaves an imbalance to correct.

"I've seen a heap of trouble in my life,
and most of it never came to pass."
MARK TWAIN

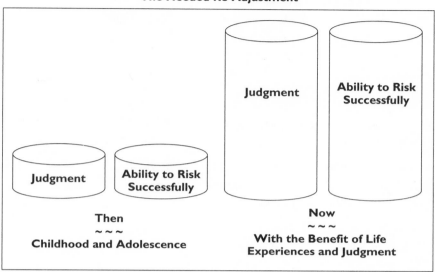

The Needed Re-Adjustment

As illustrated above, you now have a vital tool you didn't have back then—far better judgment.

BRAIN DEVELOPMENT AND JUDGMENT

The idea that you have better judgment now than as a child or adolescent may seem intuitively valid. But because setting aside risk avoidance conditioning from that period of your life is such an important part of improving your ability to risk successfully, let's look at research that supports this assertion beyond a shadow of a doubt.

Those who have teenagers now or a clear memory of their own teen years will tell you that their judgment during those years was—to be kind—inconsistent. For years, the assumption of medical science has been that the surge of hormonal activity in the teen years caused them to have flawed judgment. This is accurate. Research shows that hormonal activity during those years is particularly active in the brain's emotional center, the limbic system, resulting in what Ronald Dahl, M.D., a psychiatrist at the University of Pittsburgh, calls a "tinderbox of emotions."[8]

> **Hormonal activity during teen years is particularly active in the brain's emotional center, the limbic system, resulting in a "tinderbox of emotions."**

Other factors lead to variable judgment during adolescence. Jay Giedd, M.D., the Chief of Brain Imaging at the Child Psychiatry Branch of the National Institute of Mental Health, has conducted extensive research on the developmental process of the brain during the teen years. He concludes that "the brain of teenagers is not completely developed ... one of the last parts of the brain to complete the maturation process is the prefrontal cortex, the part of the brain responsible for planning, judgment and self-control."[9]

Dr. Giedd also observed that "it's sort of unfair to expect teens to have adult levels of organizational skills or decision making before their brain is finished being built."[10] Hence, we didn't!

Medical research affirms what we suspected—that our judgment was variable and still developing during our adolescence. Yet that's when our relationship with risk-taking was likely established. Since adolescence has passed, let's redefine that relationship now.

THE ACTION STEP

Think of something you now do well that was a struggle when you first tried it. For me, writing is a good example. For the first 40 years of my life, I considered my writing skills to be substandard. Only recently have I worked hard to develop them. What was a real challenge for you at first, but now you feel you've accomplished it well? It could be riding a bicycle, cooking, woodworking—anything involving your improved talents.

Now, with that capability in mind, ask yourself this question. What if, after it did not go well the first time you tried it, you had just decided it was something you could never do? Obviously, you would have limited yourself needlessly and missed opportunities ever since.

So revisit your perception of risk, set aside irrelevant remnants of your early conditioning, wipe the slate clean from negative past experiences, and start fresh. You now have the knowledge of an adult who has far better judgment than an adolescent. As such, you have a much greater ability to risk successfully.

> **Revisit your perception of risk, set aside irrelevant remnants of your early conditioning, wipe the slate clean from negative past experiences, and start fresh. You now have the knowledge of an adult who has far better judgment than an adolescent.**

"To dare is to lose your footing momentarily.
To not dare is to lose yourself."
SOREN KIERKEGAARD

OUR FRIEND FEAR

There is a second reason I'm bringing up the risk avoidance temptation—that is, the fear response inherent in pursuing opportunities and taking risks. There is a strong temptation to let the fear that commonly and naturally occurs when we consider a risk keep us from going forward. I don't want that to happen to you.

> **There is a strong temptation to let the fear that commonly occurs when we consider a risk keep us from going forward.**

Managing fear is a vital part of taking risks successfully. This is so important, it's the sole topic of Chapter 9. For now, I want to make these two quick comments about managing fear so you don't let it keep you from continuing.

- **Fear is natural, normal, and healthy.** Don't be concerned if, at some point in this discussion, you feel a twinge of fear. That's perfectly appropriate. I would even say it is good. It means you are serious about improving your risking-taking skills.

- **Fear comes in two forms.** These are *Emotional Fears* that are gut driven and instinctive, and *Mental Fears* that are mind driven and rational. Both are powerful. This process will help you minimize your Emotional Fear and learn from your Mental Fear. So if you're experiencing some fear, hang in there. Be confident you're right on target.

The Fears

DISCOVER YOUR LATENT COURAGE

In Chapter 1, you did an exercise called *Your Turning Points*. Let's go back to what you wrote in the three columns. The first column is Turning Point, the second column is Risks Taken, and the third column is untitled and blank. Please retrieve it and label the third column "Why I Took the Risk."

Positive Self-Determined Turning Points

Turning Point	Risks Taken	Why I Took the Risk

These are your next steps:

1. One at a time, and with focused thought, look at each Turning Point and recall again the circumstances surrounding that event.

2. Now look at what you identified as the risks you took to create that Turning Point.

3. With all this foremost in your mind, ask, "Why did I take that risk? What led me to it? What was my motivation?"

This was a special, and possibly even extraordinary, time in your life. You took a risk that may have been unusual for you. The courage to take that risk came from you. It was within you and you called on it. Set aside your humility, give yourself credit for the courage you exhibited in taking that risk, and examine why you did it.

Set aside your humility, give yourself credit for the courage you exhibited in taking that risk.

No one else needs to see this exercise. You will not have to defend what you write to anyone. Give yourself credit for being courageous and write what inspired you in the "Why I Took the Risk" column.

AN EXAMPLE TO ASSIST YOU

It might be helpful to have an example. Instead of coming up with a hypothetical one, I'll draw from my actual circumstances.

An important Turning Point in my life was when I landed a job I had long sought. It was a highly desired position that I had worked toward for many years. Years before, I had developed a strategy for getting myself qualified for such a position. Interim steps included a certain sequence of jobs so I would acquire the needed experience and additional topic-specific education to further qualify me. In this case, it was a master's degree in business administration with an emphasis in finance and marketing.

With my graduate studies nearing completion, and my resume current and crisp, I set about the classic networking process of getting in the door with prospective employers. The position I was seeking was not the kind advertised in the newspaper or anywhere else. This required getting referred from one person to the next to the next.

After I had been at it awhile with only limited results, I was getting frustrated. I knew what I wanted. I knew that, given the opportunity, I could do it well. But I had not yet found any decision makers willing to take a chance on me.

Through a referral, I got in the door with a company I really wanted to work for. The decision makers showed interest but hesitated to make the financial commitment to bring me on board.

I was there for my third interview—I remember it like it was yesterday. The person I was interviewing with was one of the two decision makers. He was going on and on about how it was hard for them to justify the cost of bringing me on without the projects in hand to keep me busy and generate revenue.

After he had come up with all the reasons he could think of not to hire me, I shifted to the front edge of my chair, leaned toward him across his large desk, and became fairly animated. I said, "I belong here. My energy and abilities are the perfect complement to your experience, connections, and access to capital. I am so convinced I belong here that I'm willing to work without pay until I find a project to your liking that will support my salary. I'll wait tables at night if that's what it takes to make this happen."

His eyes got about the size of silver dollars. He didn't know what to say. He excused himself and went down the hall to talk with the other decision maker. I stood up, looked around his gracious office, and thought I may have taken this too far. At this point, I was certainly frustrated having pursued a position for months with no results. And I knew this was exactly the setting I wanted to be in. I was ready to take a risk.

Within 24 hours, we established an agreement for me to start with this company. I was successful at finding a project within a few weeks and ended up working for six years, ultimately becoming a vice president of the company.

So here is what my exercise looks like for this Turning Point.

Turning Point	Risk Taken	Why I Took the Risk
Landing first job after completion of graduate school	*Risked not being paid for a while and having to take a second job to support myself* *Risked the whole idea falling flat and having to do something else*	*Goal Clarity—certainty of the kind of job I was seeking* *Good Match—confident this job was a good match for my skills and training* *Frustration—my frustration at having so little to show for my many months of effort seeking this type of position*

ANOTHER EXAMPLE TO ASSIST YOU

My first skydive proved to be an extremely important Turning Point in my life. I had no idea at the time that it would even be a Turning Point. We often don't. Only many years later did I realize what a significant Turning Point it was.

My first skydive was a Turning Point because it led to my second skydive and my third and my fourth and then thousands. I went on to become a professional skydiver. Skydiving has had a profoundly positive effect on my confidence and self-image. Because I'm an accomplished skydiver, I was a candidate to be a member of an expedition that sought to skydive to the North Pole. I joined the expedition and we were successful. My first skydive was also the first step towards earning World Records in the sport.

You can see how my first skydive was a critical Turning Point. However, at the time, I saw it as nothing more than an exciting one-time experience and the completion of a long-held goal.

I have a strong need for control. I seek to have a lot of influence on the outcome of events in my life. At times, this is an attribute. At times, it puts limits on my personal achievement. This control need definitely qualifies as one of those Strength/Weakness Paradox items mentioned in Chapter 3.

To make a skydive, you have to accept that there is a possibility of outcomes you cannot control. Some of those outcomes would be negative and in a worse case could include your death.

While losing your life on your first skydive is exceedingly unlikely, it's possible. But it's also possible that a quick trip to the supermarket could result in a fatal accident. Without citing the statistical likelihood of either, my point is that *almost every activity has the potential for a negative outcome*—even those that seem pretty safe.

For example, I heard in the news about a deranged gunman who burst into a church service on a Sunday morning and fatally shot some worshipers. While this was a horribly tragic event, it definitely makes the point that no activity is without risk. For the people who lost their lives, the honorable and seemingly benign act of going to church on a Sunday morning was their final act.

When you decide to experience the exhilaration and beauty of a sky-dive, you have to trust people you've only just met, equipment you don't fully understand, and your own good fortune. For a person like me with a strong control need, that was a real challenge. I had to find courage somewhere to do this jump!

I had put a lot of thought into taking my first skydive. I took that risk because, for me, the rewards justified it—that is, what I hoped would be a wonderful and meaningful experience justified taking the small but real risk of injury or death. A calculation like this doesn't have anything to do with anyone else. For me, it made sense.

A second reason I took the risk was that I wanted to prove to myself that I could squarely face a significant fear and move past it. I wanted to bolster my confidence.

Here's how my Turning Point exercise reads for this experience.

Turning Point	Risk Taken	Why I Took the Risk
First skydive	*Trusted my safety to instructors, equipment, my ability, and fate*	*Rewards—a unique life experience and the confidence I hoped to gain*

I'm pleased to tell you it worked. Doing my first skydive *did* bolster my confidence. To this day, I can remember driving home thinking, "If I can do *that*, I can do anything." In my adrenaline-drenched state, my logic was obviously not at its best, but you see my point. I genuinely felt more confident.

I experienced a second huge benefit. This one was more subtle but also more significant. My willingness to accept my inability to prevail in the face of possible negative outcomes was also a Turning Point. In a rare moment, I had voluntarily accepted a lack of control. As usual with Turning Points, I didn't realize it was one at the time. But my first skydive turned out to be a critical first step in lessening my performance-limiting control need.

GIVE YOURSELF CREDIT

So get to it. Go back through your Turning Point exercise and fill in your Why I Took the Risk, column. Be thoughtful. Don't rush. The more you put into it, the more you'll get out of it. More important insights await!

Critical Step

Before you go on, fully complete this Turning Points exercise.

Once you've completed this exercise, set it in front of you. Focus on the second and third columns. Look at the risks you've taken and why you took them. *None of these* happened without some courage. *You exhibited courage!* Give yourself credit for it. Are you seeing evidence of courage you don't commonly acknowledge? Don't minimize your actions and courage. On that piece of paper is evidence of courage you may not have given yourself credit for having. Take credit for it now.

This is important stuff. Chances are you have been underrating your courage. Please catch yourself if you find you're saying, "Well, that situation was different. Those were unique circumstances." Fine. That may be true. But the courage was present and it will be again when you're ready to call on it.

You have exhibited courage in the past. Give yourself credit for having it and keep its presence within you foremost in your mind as we move forward.

Seizing opportunities is going to require you to take some risks, which will demand that you draw on your courage. As this exercise shows, you have courage within you because you've exhibited it in the past. Give yourself credit for having it and keep its presence within you foremost in your mind as we move forward.

> *"Our doubts are traitors and make us lose the*
> *good we oft might win by fearing to attempt."*
> WILLIAM SHAKESPEARE

On-Line Tool

A Turning Points exercise that provides you with a consolidated version of the steps assessing past Turning Points and your motivation, as you have done earlier in Chapter 1 and continued in this chapter, is available at *www.TakeRisks.com/tools.*

CHAPTER 5

Your Passion and Calling

Chances are you have things you feel passionate about. Being aware of and respecting these passions will help you take risks and pursue opportunities more successfully.

YOUR PASSION/LIFE NEXUS

> *"If you do not feel yourself growing in your work*
> *and your life broadening and deepening,*
> *if your task is not a perpetual tonic to you,*
> *you have not found your place."*
> ORISON SWETT MARDEN

Self-awareness can be frightening. It can confront you with bothersome questions.

As we advance through our lives, we become more aware of where our true passions lie. As we mature, our priorities change. When you add changing interests and priorities to the kind of discoveries you're hopefully making as you proceed through this book, you have the potential for coming to some uncomfortable realizations.

As we advance through our lives, we become more aware of where our true passions lie. As we mature, our priorities change.

You may see your Passions and Natural Skill Set taking you in one direction and your career and Life Structure taking you in another. Has the work you deeply cared about at one time become uninspiring? Do you find you are tolerating your job because the money you make allows you to do the things you really care about? Or it just pays the bills? Is there a big gap between what you've come to realize you're ideally suited for and what you do? Have the commitments you've made in your life become obstacles that keep you from pursuing your Passion?

If the answer to any or all of these questions is yes, rejoice! Coming to these realizations is the first step toward breaking down barriers between your passions and your current Life Structure. Until you acknowledge the existence of your barriers, you won't have much success dismantling them.

You may be living the all-too-common "cupcake pan existence." What's that? Think of a cupcake pan with the separate indentions for each cupcake. Your passions are in one part, your priorities are in another, and your job is in yet another. They're not intermixed.

The goal is to combine them. This means getting your life out of the "cupcake pan" model and into a "cake pan" model. Just like a cake mix, you want everything in your life to blend together well. It may not be perfect when you're done, but it will be better. There will be more of a blending of your Passion, Priorities, Occupation, and Life Structure.

Martin Seligman, a psychologist at the University of Pennsylvania and authority on the science of happiness, says that becoming more engaged in what you do is one of the three components of happiness. The other two are finding ways to make your life more meaningful and getting more pleasure out of your life.[11]

Becoming more engaged in what you do is one of the three components of happiness.

Your goal is to move toward a *Passion/Life Nexus*. A nexus is simply a connection or link between different things. You want to build and strengthen the connection between your passion and how you live your life. The stronger your nexus, the better you'll be at taking risks and pursuing opportunities.

Tapping into your passion has a profound effect. Think about the times you've taken on tasks you felt passionately about. Do you see how it's entirely different than handling tasks that don't excite you?

When you're on a course fueled by passion you're energized.

When you're on a course fueled by passion you're energized. Naturally, you'll always have responsibilities you must respect that don't provide a passion connection. That's unavoidable. But by being aware of your passions and pursuing opportunities consistent with them when possible, you'll do yourself a great favor. You'll tap into additional energy that will increase your chances of succeeding.

> *"The person who does not work for the love of work but only for money is not likely to make money nor to find much fun in life."*
> CHARLES SCHWAB

Your Purpose, Calling, Dream Job, Life Structure, and Other Powerful Concepts

Natural Skill Set and Passion are powerful concepts. To make this conversation more interesting, let's add Purpose, Calling, Dream Job, and Life Structure.

Being aware of your Natural Skill Set, Passions, Purpose, Calling, Dream Job and Life Structure will assist you.

You might be thinking, "What does this have to do with risk-taking?" A great deal. But this is not a book about discerning your Life Purpose. Many good books on that topic are readily available. Because these concepts relate to improving your risk-taking and opportunity-seizing talents, being aware of them and how they relate to each other will assist you.

The resulting message is this:

- The more you are aware of your innate talents, driving passions, and Life Purpose to the extent you have identified them, the better you will be at successfully exploiting opportunities.

- This will occur by leveraging your awareness of these aspects of who you are in the opportunities you pursue and the decisions you make.

Let's quickly describe these concepts.

Concept	Description	Comments
Natural Skill Set	Your innate talents	Readily identifiable with a little effort
Passions	Your deeply held desires, concerns, and beliefs	Readily identifiable with a little effort, important to be aware of them, affect you profoundly
Purpose	Your perception of your reason for being	Powerful, elusive, and evolving—a heady concept that can be difficult to identify
Calling	The role your Natural Skill Set, Passions, and Purpose all lead you to	Another powerful but possibly elusive concept
Dream Job	The job you love so much that you would almost do it without pay	Much different than an easy job that demands little of you
Life Structure	The extent to which you have incorporated all these concepts into your day-to-day life	The more you have, the better you will be at selecting opportunities and taking risks

As you can see, these concepts are all distinct but related.

**If you read the Natural Skill Set exercise
but did not actually do it, I encourage
you to go back *now* and complete it.**

You already identified your Natural Skill Set in Chapter 3. If you read the exercise but did not actually do it, I encourage you to go back *now* and complete it. You owe it to yourself. Again, what you get out of this book will be determined by what you put into it.

IDENTIFY YOUR PASSIONS

> *"Without passion man is a mere latent force and*
> *possibility, like the flint which awaits the shock*
> *of the iron before it can give forth its spark."*
> HENRI FREDERIC AMIEL

Your Passions can be readily discerned. If you cannot readily identify them, simply answering these questions:
- What is most important to me?
- What would I sacrifice almost everything else for?
- What in my life would I give up last if I had to choose?

Your answers to these questions will get you close to knowing your Passions. The next step is to ask a few people who know you well what they see as your passions (as you did in Chapter 3 when identifying your Natural Skill Set).

A Warning About Passions

Passions are a powerful driving force that need to be respected and treated with caution.

Passions are a powerful driving force that need to be respected and treated with caution.

That is why it is vital that you're aware of yours.

Remember the Strength/Weakness Paradox in Chapter 3? The lesson was that any positive trait, if applied in the extreme, can become negative.

Passions have the same potential. They can inspire you to do wonderful things for yourself and others. They can drive you to great achievements. Clearly, they serve you well to a point. But they can also serve you poorly. They can drag you down and drive you to unproductive or even discrediting behavior.

This is why, as with all of these concepts, gaining awareness is the critical first step. Until you're consciously aware of your Passions, you have no ability to harness them and rein them in, if necessary, for your own benefit.

Awareness is key.

PURPOSE AND CALLING

> *"We are not here merely to make a living. We*
> *are here to enrich the world, and we impoverish*
> *ourselves if we forget this errand."*
> WOODROW WILSON

You'll likely find that Purpose and Calling are harder to discern than Natural Skill Set and Passions. Many people never do identify them. Identifying yours requires self-awareness likely preceded by a good deal of self-examination and probably the wisdom of at least a few decades of life. You may be among the few with clarity of Purpose and Calling earlier in your life than most. That is a great joy. If this is the case, keep in mind that, as with all these concepts, your Purpose and Calling can change as you progress though life.

**I encourage you to put thought into big
questions like the role for which you are
uniquely suited and why you've been given
space and oxygen here on earth.**

Please don't be concerned if you're thinking, "I have no clue what either my Purpose or Calling is." That's common. You gain value from spending time thinking about them, even if you're not clear on exactly what they are. As you continue, I encourage you to put thought into big questions like the role for which you are uniquely suited and why you've been given space and oxygen here on earth. There is no harm in entertaining such thoughts.

Should you gain clarity about your Purpose and Calling, you'll have a great gift and powerful tool. Being aware of either or both will help you discern what risks to take and which opportunities to pursue.

A Warning About Your Calling

As mentioned earlier, self-awareness can be frightening. It can also be a mixed blessing. While it's a great joy to be aware of your Calling, it can also create a heavy burden. Once you become aware of your Calling, you'll find that pursuing any tasks and roles inconsistent with your Calling will become increasingly difficult.

Being aware of your Calling gives you clear direction, but it also burdens you with the responsibility of fulfilling it. I feel very fortunate that I'm aware of mine. but I'm also often reminded of the responsibilities my Calling places on me. Pursing a course that is inconsistent with your Calling can be both difficult and dispiriting.

This wise thought from 20th-century psychologist and motivational theory innovator Abraham Maslow comes to mind:

"A musician must make music,
an artist must paint,
a poet must write.
If he is to be ultimately at peace with himself,
what a man can be he must be."
ABRAHAM MASLOW

What if you're aware of your Calling and concerned that it's not something that allows you to make a living? No problem. Fulfilling your Calling may have little to do with your occupation.

**Fulfilling your Calling may have little
to do with your occupation.**

For example, take those who know their Calling is to provide care and love to animals, but their finances require them to work in an unrelated field. They can fulfill it by volunteering at the local animal shelter, being active in the Humane Society, joining local animal rescue efforts, offering emergency shelter for animals at their home, organizing low-cost spay and neuter clinics, and getting involved in animal adoption activities.

At some time, they may be able to retire or live on less income. Then they can fulfill their Calling differently, such as by taking a paid position at an animal shelter or a veterinary clinic or becoming a fundraiser for the Humane Society. Whether it's their vocation or avocation, they are fulfilling their Calling.

"Do what you can, with what you have, where you are."
THEODORE ROOSEVELT

MAKE YOUR MARK

If you know your Calling, you owe it to yourself to pursue it. This doesn't mean quitting your job tomorrow to pursue your Calling based on nothing but hope that things will work out. As with the entire process of seizing opportunities successfully, you need to be thoughtful before making your move. But you do need to pursue your Calling in some way. Anything less will leave your mark unmade.

AWARENESS LEADING TO FULFILLMENT

As mentioned earlier, your important first step is becoming aware of your Natural Skill Set, your Passion, your Purpose, and your Calling. That's key. Your second step is to honor them.

Respect your natural strengths and limitations when selecting which risks to take, which opportunities to pursue, and making important decisions.

Respect your natural strengths and limitations when selecting which risks to take, which opportunities to pursue, and making important decisions. By doing so, something wonderful will happen. You will find they become more central in your life.

You may have to accept some differences between your guiding tenets and Life Structure. They may be only temporary and with time you can bring them into alignment. Step by step, you'll become more successful with the risks you take and feel more fulfilled as a result.

Again, these three steps are:

1. Becoming aware of your Strengths, Limitations, Passions, Calling, and Purpose to the extent they have become clear to you.

2. Respecting these innate elements of who you are when you make decisions large and small.

3. Moving, perhaps gradually, to incorporate these personal elements into your Life Structure.

Doing so will not only make you better at taking risks, but you'll experience recurring joy and fulfillment as a result.

"The greatest discovery of any generation
is that a human being can alter his
life by altering his attitudes."
WILLIAM JAMES

CHAPTER 6

Identifying the Opportunity

To this point, we've focused on improving your opportunity-seizing and risk-taking skills. Now let's apply these improved skills. Since it's impossible to pursue an opportunity until you identify it, that's the next step.

THE SPECTRUM OF ALL RISKS

All the risks you could consider—from the most extreme to the most benign—fit into one of three categories: Chosen, Optional, and Avoided. From the most extreme risk—base jumping off the Empire State Building with a deteriorating parachute on a stormy day—to the most benign such as getting out of bed, all fit into one of these three categories.

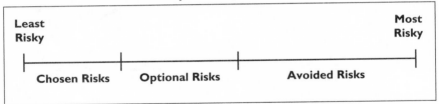

The Spectrum of All Risks

CHOSEN RISKS

As discussed earlier, risk is an unavoidable part of our lives. We can't function effectively without taking some risks, even if we'd prefer not to. Risks that are required to function (whether you like them or not) are *Chosen Risks*.

You may not even think of Chosen Risks as risks because they are so common in your life.

You may not even think of Chosen Risks as risks because they are so common in your life. Your daily transportation is a good example of a Chosen Risk.

Whether your primary means of daily transportation is car, public transportation, or walking, all pose risks. While you may not have actually analyzed the risks presented by your daily transportation, you have still effectively made a decision to accept the risks they present. Being able to get from one place to the next is likely required for you to effectively function. As such, you have decided that your means of daily transportation is a Chosen Risk.

OPTIONAL RISKS

"Life is either always a tightrope or a feather bed.
Give me the tightrope."
Edith Wharton

Optional Risks are risks you've chosen to take even though they're not mandatory for you to function. You could get by without taking them, but you have chosen, for any number of reasons, to take them. An Optional Risk would be drinking water from the tap in a place where drinking bottled water is known to be safer or choosing to fly someplace instead of staying home.

Here's a detailed example of an Optional Risk. Consider a person whose workplace is on the other side of a major river from where they live. As they commute to and from work every day, they have a choice of four different ways to get there:

Option 1: Crossing via a major bridge that rises high above the river to accommodate ship traffic,

Option 2: Crossing via a drawbridge that isn't nearly as high above the water, but is out of the way and adds many miles to the commute,

Option 3: Crossing via an auto ferry that is slow and unreliable, and

Option 4: Crossing via train service, with the nearest station being five miles from where they live and one mile from where they work.

Add to equation the fact that this person fears heights, so they really dislike being on the major bridge that rises high above the river. Let's also assume that traveling over the major bridge can be shown to be one of the riskier options. Yet this person has chosen to commute over the high major bridge because it is the fastest way to get to and from work. This means taking the bridge route is an Optional Risk.

The fact that you have not consciously analyzed the options before taking action does not make it less of a risk.

In all these situations, a risk—no matter how slight—is being taken. The fact that you have not consciously analyzed the options before taking action does not make it less of a risk. It just means you took the risk naturally and instinctively.

AVOIDED RISKS

Avoided Risks are those that, at any given time, you deem unnecessary or undesirable for your normal functioning. The risks that are in your Avoided category at any given time are variable. Here is an example of how Avoided Risks can vary.

The risks in your Avoided category at any given time are variable, not fixed.

Many people make dating an Avoided Risk at certain times in their lives. They may have had an emotionally painful experience in a relationship and decided the possibility of more emotional pain makes dating an undesirable risk.

You know the scenario. Someone is dating a person who doesn't turn out to be as thoughtful, caring, loyal, or single as they thought. Their feelings get hurt. The relationship ends. Emotional scars accumulate and the person declares, "I've had it with dating. They're all jerks. I would rather sit home Saturday night and watch TV than go through that again."

For that person, dating has become, for now, an Avoided Risk. After some time, dating again becomes an Optional Risk for most people. The emotional scars heal and they start dating.

Then there are Avoided Risks that have always been (and will likely always be) Avoided Risks. They may be things that make no sense to you and you'll never choose to make them Optional Risks. Often, these permanent Avoided Risks fall in the area of physical risks. For example, a friend of mine has no interest in snow skiing because he perceives the risk of getting injured as being too great. For him, skiing is a permanent Avoided Risk.

WHERE TO FIND OPPORTUNITIES

Naturally, your list of Avoided Risks changes and the dividing line between your Optional Risks and Avoided Risks moves. As you shift a few risks out of Avoided and into Optional, the line moves right. You've become bolder. You've increased the area on the Spectrum of Risks that falls into Optional. Conversely, if Optional Risks become Avoided Risks, the line moves left.

That all-important line between Optional and Avoided Risks is your threshold, the edge of your abyss, the boundary of your Comfort Zone, your frontier. It is your *Comfort Threshold*.

Let's focus on that all-important line between Optional and Avoided Risks. This is your threshold, the edge of your abyss, the boundary of your Comfort Zone. This is where, for now, you've drawn your own line in the sand. This is your frontier, what we call your *Comfort Threshold*.

The Critical Line Between Optional Risks and Avoided Risks
Your Comfort Threshold

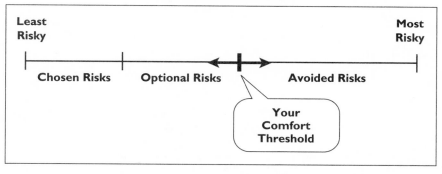

On the right side of the line, in Avoided Risks, are risks that will never make sense for you and a few that might someday, just not now. Think of standing next to a solid fence up on your toes so you can just barely see over it. On the other side of the fence are all of your Avoided Risks. Looking over this figurative "fence" can be a frightening proposition.

On the other side of this "fence" are things you've decided to avoid. If you find the risks on your Avoided list particularly threatening, you may have put a lot of effort into building a rather substantial "fence"—one that's strong and tall. Just looking over the "fence" may be a sweaty palms proposition for you.

It is just over that "fence"—right there among your Avoided Risks—that you're most likely to find your opportunities. This is your *Opportunity Territory*.

Why all the emphasis on the line between your Optional and Avoided Risks? Why focus on this figurative fence at the edge of your Comfort Zone? Because it is just over that "fence"—right there among your Avoided Risks—that you're most likely to find your opportunities. This is your *Opportunity Territory*.

Venturing into your Opportunity Territory will involve taking risks and will probably take you out of your Comfort Zone. That is why the first five chapters of this book focus on improving your risk-taking skills. The better you are at it, the less frightening it will be.

Where You Will Find the Opportunities

Where specifically will you find the right opportunities to pursue? Everywhere. In fact, as you become more open to pursuing them, you'll find them being presented to you regularly.

In the workplace, they'll come in the form of special projects, position openings, topic-specific task forces, relocation opportunities, and more.

Your challenge will be less in identifying them than in being discerning when determining which ones to take.

In your community, opportunities will include volunteer positions, perhaps political involvement, assisting or becoming an elected official, leadership and service opportunities in civic and church organizations, and much more.

In the entrepreneurial and investment realm, you'll find them everywhere once you start looking for them. There is never any shortage of people seeking investment capital. And business opportunities abound for people willing to invest the time and money to exploit such opportunities. Again, the challenge is not in *recognizing* the opportunities but in finding the ones that match your Passions and Natural Skill Set.

The challenge is not in *recognizing* the opportunities but in finding the ones that match your Passions and Natural Skill Set.

What will all these opportunities have in common? They will almost certainly, in some way, take you beyond the current limits of your Comfort Zone.

But don't worry. The rest of this book provides you with tools to help you evaluate opportunities, manage fear and uncertainty, and maximize the chances of success once you're underway.

Before getting into those topics, let's spend a little time helping you become even more discerning in your approach to pursuing opportunities and balancing the risks involved.

HOW SITUATIONS INFLUENCE YOUR WILLINGNESS TO RISK

The position of your Comfort Threshold on the Risk Spectrum moves just like your RQ. They are both influenced by your circumstances at a given moment. This means they are *situational*.

Your Comfort Threshold on the Risk Spectrum and your RQ are both influenced by your circumstances at a given moment.

This is part of the reason a certain risk may be on your Avoided Risks list one month and on your Optional Risks list the next. Some circumstances can make you more risk inclined and expand your Optional Risks. Dramatic ones can include finding yourself in an emergency or disaster situation. Confronted with an extraordinary situation, you may respond in an extraordinary, out-of-character way.

Other situations that may make you more risk inclined and cause you to move both your Comfort Threshold and RQ to the right include a high level of dissatisfaction. Being extremely unhappy can inspire you to take risks beyond your normal pattern. A need to increase your income so you can honor commitments can lead you to launch a new venture or start a new job.

Similarly, certain situations can make you less risk inclined and have the effect of moving your Comfort Threshold and RQ to the left. Becoming a parent, for example, can have that effect. A personal or professional setback can do the same, but hopefully only temporarily.

A job loss is a situation that can move you in either direction. I've seen people respond to a job loss by becoming more risk inclined; they welcome it as an opportunity to seek a more satisfying job or go to work for themselves. I have also observed people becoming less risk inclined and more cautious due to a job loss.

Here are the key points in all this:

1. Your Comfort Threshold and your RQ are situational.
2. Just because something is beyond your Comfort Threshold today does not mean it will always be.
3. Something that is on your Avoided Risks list today can be on your Optional Risks list in the future.

The way it is today does not have to be the
way it is going to always be for you.
Things change.
JIM McCORMICK

ACTUAL RISK VERSUS PERCEIVED RISK

Another important awareness for you is that there can be a big difference between what you *perceive* as the risk being taken and the actual risk itself. This happens because the person or organization taking the risk may have gone to great lengths to mitigate any negative outcomes from the risk in ways that aren't apparent.

Here's an example. Envision two boats leaving a harbor for a day of ocean fishing. You're viewing them from a bluff above the harbor. From that vantage point, they look nearly identical. They are the same size and configured similarly. Both have two people on board and lots of fishing poles.

From all appearances, they are taking identical risks. Certainly, a day of ocean fishing comes with potential risks. The weather can change suddenly. The boat can have mechanical problems. People in the boat can experience a medical emergency. Thick vision-obscuring fog can roll in. Large waves can build. Plenty of other potential problems can occur.

Now here's where the difference between Perceived Risks and Actual Risks occurs.

One of the seemingly identical boats is equipped with a Global Positioning System (GPS) receiver, radar, and current navigational charts. The other has none of these.

The boat with the navigational equipment also has a ship-to-shore radio and a fully charged cell phone as a back up. The other boat has neither.

The well-equipped boat also has a back-up outboard engine, an emergency fuel tank, and a main engine that was recently serviced. It has new life preservers, an inflatable life raft, survival supplies including emergency water and food, a flare gun to signal for assistance, and an extensive first aid kit. The poorly equipped boat has none of these.

The person at the wheel of the well-equipped boat has taken marine safety and navigation classes and recently participated in man-overboard training conducted by the Coast Guard.

The person steering the poorly equipped boat is using the boat for the first time, having borrowed it from a friend. He has only boated on lakes before, but figures navigating in the ocean can't be much different than in a lake.

The person in the well-equipped boat obtained the most recent weather reports before departing, then she informed a friend (both verbally and in writing) of her plans and anticipated return time. Her friend agreed to notify the Coast Guard and the Harbor Police if she was not back by the return time.

The well-equipped mariner is a classic example of taking a risk and minimizing its possible negative outcomes.

The fellow piloting the poorly equipped boat told no one of his plans, but he does have a six-pack of beer and a few peanut butter and jelly sandwiches.

Who is taking the greater risk? I guess you could say that, strictly speaking, both are taking identical risks. But clearly those on the well-equipped boat are much more likely to return safely from a day on the ocean. Yet, it's important to note that, from your perspective watching from the bluff above the harbor, both boats appear to be taking the same risks.

The well-equipped mariner is a classic example of minimizing the possible negative outcomes of taking a risk. This example is important for two reasons:

1. It reminds us that there may be much more we need to know before we decide if a certain course of action is acceptable. Joining

one of these boats for a day of ocean fishing without finding out about their level of preparation would be a bad idea.

2. We can do a great deal to increase the chances of a positive outcome and reduce the chances of a negative outcome. This is such an important element in taking risks and pursuing opportunities that all of Chapter 8 is dedicated to it.

> *"It is the business of the future to be dangerous."*
> ALFRED NORTH WHITEHEAD

TIME TO ROLL UP YOUR SLEEVES

I hope your ability to recognize opportunities has been enhanced, perhaps significantly. You've put some thought into your risk inclination—your Comfort Threshold and RQ—changing at times. And you've been reminded that a surface assessment of both an opportunity and a risk is almost never enough to allow you to make a good decision.

It's time to roll up your sleeves and apply your knowledge and insights to analyzing specific opportunities. That's what we're doing next.

> *"Inaction breeds doubt and fear.*
> *Action breeds confidence and courage.*
> *If you want to conquer fear, do not*
> *sit home and think about it.*
> *Go out and get busy."*
> DALE CARNEGIE

CHAPTER 7

Evaluating the Opportunity

U p to this point, we've focused on improving your abil-ity to take risks and pursue opportunities by increasing your awareness of your natural gifts and passions. You have also gained insights that will help you recognize opportunities.

To continue this process, we need to assume that you've identified an opportunity and have an interest in pursuing it. Thoughtfully analyzing the opportunity and the risks involved is the next step. In this and the next chapter, you will be given a eight-step process for assessing opportunities and enhancing the chances of a successful outcome.

On-Line Tool

A Risk Assessment/Success Enhancement (RASE) tool that provides you with a consolidated version of the eight assessments and decision steps contained in this and the next chapter is available at *www.TakeRisks.com/tools.*

IDENTIFY THE OPPORTUNITY

"Before beginning a hunt, it is wise to
ask someone what you are looking for
before you begin looking for it."
POOH'S LITTLE INSTRUCTION BOOK
INSPIRED BY A.A. MILNE

First, describe the opportunity in writing. Your description needs to be brief and as specific as possible. Doing this will keep you focused on exactly what you're evaluating. The following sentences are good examples of how to state opportunities:

- Relocate this fall to central Florida.
- Start evening classes next month to complete a college degree.
- Introduce a new awards program within your team at work.
- Enroll in graduate school this year.
- Start pursuing a new position with your current employer.
- Reorganize your work team to better respond to client needs.
- Accept the job offer you've received for the _____ position with _____ company.
- Buy a new, more reliable car.

And here are examples of how *not* to state opportunities:

- Move out of this area.
- Figure out how to improve profitability.
- Think about taking some college classes.
- Motivate your colleagues.
- See if there are apartments you like better than the one you live in now.

Being as specific as possible will make it easier to evaluate the opportunity and increase the value of the results.

Example

We'll use an ongoing example as we go through this process. For this example, you're pursuing a new position with your current employer, so start by stating the opportunity clearly.

EXAMPLE

Step 1—Identify the Risk

Specifically State the Opportunity You are Going to Evaluate

Pursue new position with my current employer

Now, it's your turn. Write down the opportunity you're going to evaluate.

Step 1—Identify the Risk

Specifically State the Opportunity You Want to Evaluate:

_____

_____

IDENTIFY POSSIBLE OUTCOMES

Let's take a look at the likely results of seeking the position you have in mind. By pursuing this opportunity, you're taking action. Your action will result in an outcome. You don't know for certain what that outcome will be. At a minimum, there are two possible outcomes—a Best Case Outcome and a Worst Case Outcome.

The Best Case Outcome would be exactly that—the best case. It may not be ideal or perfect, but it's the best you could realistically hope for. The Worst Case Outcome is the just that. It may not be likely, but it still needs to be identified.

In addition to the Best Case and Worst Case Outcomes, there are likely some Intermediate Outcomes. An Intermediate Outcome is a result that in not best and not worst; it is something in-between.

There may be no Intermediate Outcomes. You may be considering an opportunity that has only two possible outcomes—a Best Case and a Worst Case. But there likely are some Intermediate Outcomes. In fact, there may be *many* of them.

I encourage you to limit the Intermediate Outcomes to no more than three. Three Intermediate Outcomes plus a Best Case Outcome and a Worst Case Outcome will give you five possible outcomes. Trying to assess more than five can become complex. So unless you absolutely have to consider more than five outcomes, I recommend against it.

Example

Let's continue with evaluating the opportunity of pursuing a new position with your current employer. To simplify the example, let's assume that, due to an existing policy of your employer, your compensation will not be changed for a while should you move to a new position. This takes the issue of compensation out of the evaluation. While this may seem simplistic, it will help make the example more useful. The second step looks like this:

EXAMPLE

Step 2—Identify the Possible Outcomes

Possible Outcome		Outcome Number	Initial Likelihood	Improved Likelihood
Best Case	more rewarding position	# **1**	**40** %	____ %
Intermediate	equally rewarding position	# **2**	**45** %	____ %
Intermediate		# ____	____ %	____ %
Intermediate		# ____	____ %	____ %
Worst Case	less rewarding position	# **3**	**15** %	____ %
			100 %	**100** %

Next, identify the possible outcomes for the opportunity you're evaluating and write them below. From top to bottom, put them in order from most desirable to least desirable.

- Start by filling in the Best Case Outcome.
- Then write down the Worst Case Outcome.
- Now identify the Intermediate Outcomes, if any. List the most desirable Intermediate Outcome right under Best Case.
- If you have another Intermediate Outcome that is less desirable yet, list it next.
- And finally, if you have a third and still less desirable Intermediate Outcome, write it above the Worst Case Outcome.

You've now identified from two to five possible outcomes for the opportunity you're evaluating. Next, number the outcomes you've identified starting with the Best Case as #1. Just leave any unused Intermediate Outcomes blank.

Step 3—Determine the Likelihood of the Possible Outcomes

Possible Outcome		Outcome Number	Likelihood
Best Case	_____	# **1**	_____ %
Intermediate	_____	# _____	_____ %
Intermediate	_____	# _____	_____ %
Intermediate	_____	# _____	_____ %
Worst Case	_____	# _____	_____ %
			100 %

DETERMINE THE LIKELIHOOD OF THE POSSIBLE OUTCOMES

Having identified as many as five possible outcomes, put some thought into how likely each is to occur. Express the likelihood as a percentage. For example, if you think there is a 40 percent chance of Possible Outcome #1 occurring, put "40%" in the Likelihood column for that outcome. If you think there is a 10 percent chance of Possible Outcome #2 occurring, then put "10%" in the Likelihood column for that outcome. Continue until a Likelihood percentage has been assigned to each Possible Outcome.

As you think through the likelihood of each possible outcome, keep in mind that all the Likelihoods need to add up to 100%.

EXAMPLE

Step 3—Determine the Likelihood of the Possible Outcomes

Possible Outcome		Outcome Number	Likelihood
Best Case	more rewarding position	# **1**	**30** %
Intermediate	equally rewarding position	# **2**	**40** %
Intermediate		#	%
Intermediate		#	%
Worst Case	less rewarding position	# **3**	**30** %
			100 %

Now it is your turn. Go back to your list of Possible Outcomes and assign a Likelihood expressed as a percentage for each.

Step 4—Show the Likelihoods Graphically

We all assess and absorb information differently. Looking at your Possible Outcomes Matrix with the percentages assigned to the Likelihoods may be an effective way for you to process this information. If that's true, you can skip the next step. However, many people absorb information better when it's presented graphically. This next step will take the information you already have in the Possible Outcomes Matrix and present it in a graphic form that may be more useful to you.

First, starting from the left end of the Possible Outcomes Graphic, draw a bracket for Possible Outcome #1 that is as wide as the Likelihood you assigned it. In the example, if the Likelihood of Possible Outcome #1 is 30%, the bracket will go from the left end of the graphic to the third hash mark. (The distance between each hash mark represents 10 percent.)

This is how the first bracket would look in this example:

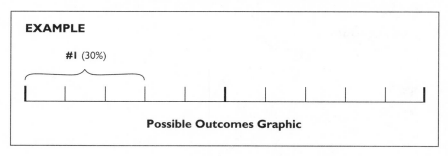

Continuing with the example, the Likelihood of Possible Outcome #2 is 40 percent and the Likelihood of Possible Outcome #3 is 30 percent. This is how the completed Possible Outcomes Graphic would look.

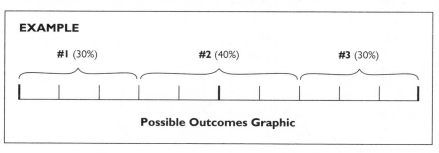

Now it's your turn. Here is the Possible Outcomes Graphic for you to complete, if you choose.

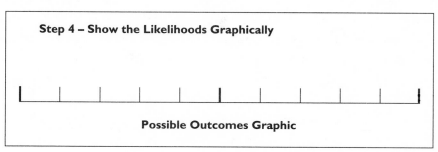

Step 5—Assess Whether to Proceed

By this point, you've put a lot of thought into the opportunity you're considering. You've identified it, estimated the Likelihoods of the Possible Outcomes, and possibly represented these outcomes graphically. Take time to step back and see what you have so far.

Do the Likelihoods seem promising enough that you are ready to move forward?

Having identified the Likelihoods of the Possible Outcomes, ask if you're ready to proceed. Do the Likelihoods seem promising enough that you are ready to move forward? Are you comfortable that the less desirable outcomes are sufficiently unlikely that you can move ahead? If so, go ahead and pursue the opportunity!

However, if you're not yet comfortable proceeding, that's not a problem. In Chapter 8, you'll be given additional steps that may make you feel more comfortable pursuing the opportunity.

"Security is mostly a superstition.
It does not exist in nature, nor do the children
of men as a whole experience it.
Avoiding danger is no safer in the long run
than outright exposure.
Life is either a daring adventure, or nothing."
HELEN KELLER

CHAPTER 8

Maximizing Your Chances of Success

"Mere precedent is a dangerous source of authority."
ANDREW JACKSON

As discussed earlier, risk is a tool to be exploited, not something to be avoided. Your goal is not to minimize the risks but to minimize the *possible negative outcomes* of the risks.

Intelligent risk-taking means leaving very little to chance and being as prepared as the mariner in the well-equipped boat from Chapter 7. This means not only doing everything possible to minimize the chances of any negative outcomes but also maximizing the chances of realizing positive outcomes.

**Intelligent risk-taking means leaving
very little to chance.**

Once you've identified and analyzed an opportunity and decided to proceed, your work has just begun. Your next step is to enhance your chances of success. Talented risk-takers don't do foolish things. Rather, they carefully assess risks before taking them and then put focused effort into maximizing their chances of success. You owe it to yourself to do the same.

Talented risk-takers don't do foolish things. They carefully assess risks before taking them and then put focused effort into maximizing their chances of success.

Put another way, taking a risk without taking steps to enhance your chances of success reduces the likelihood of a positive outcome.

Step 6—Success Enhancement

*"If you really want something
you can figure out how to make it happen."*
CHER

Continuing with the process from the last chapter, it's time to identify steps that will enhance your chances of a positive outcome. With practice, you'll learn to use this process with *any* opportunity you're considering.

With nearly every opportunity, there are steps you can take to increase the chances of a positive outcome and decrease chances of an undesirable outcome. All it takes to enjoy their benefits is to identify and take them.

These steps are called POSEMs, which stands for Possibility of Success Enhancement Measures. Simply stated, these are actions you can take to improve your chances of success.

POSEMs stands for Possibility of Success Enhancement Measures. Simply stated, these are actions you can take to improve your chances of success.

POSEMs do not have to be involved or complex. A simple POSEM to enhance the chances of a successful presentation is to reduce the chances of getting food poisoning by forgoing eating shellfish or raw fish the week before. This means I may not be able to enjoy mussels, clams, oysters, and sushi for extended periods, but it's worth it. The last thing I want is experiencing the writhing pain of food poisoning the night before presenting. While the chances of getting food poisoning from good quality raw fish are low, they are *zero* if I don't eat it at all. This is an example of a simple POSEM.

THE POWER OF POSEMs

POSEMs also make you feel more comfortable about the risk you're taking. Here's why.

Psychologist Emanuel Maidenberg, Ph.D., at the UCLA Neuropsychiatric Institute, has researched how humans respond to threats to their well being. Because we can easily see an undesirable outcome to a risk as a possible threat to our well being, Dr. Maidenberg's insights are interesting.

He observed that "as human beings we feel much more comfortable when we have more predictability and we have more control, and whether it is true control or perceived control, the outcome is pretty much the same—we do feel better about it."[12]

Clearly, POSEMs make things more predictable and hence allow you to feel more comfortable with the risk you're taking. That's powerful.

We feel much more comfortable when we have more predictability and more control, whether it is true control or perceived control.

So how do you identify POSEMs for the opportunity you are considering? By thinking broadly.

> *"We fear things in proportion to our ignorance of them."*
> TITUS LIVIUS LIVY
> ANCIENT ROMAN HISTORIAN

RESEARCH POSEMs

POSEMs can involve research. Examples include—

- Talking with people who have pursued an opportunity similar to the one you're considering. Ask if they would do it again and what they would do differently.
- Talking with people who have unsuccessfully pursued a similar idea and finding out what they would do differently.
- Learning everything you can about the opportunity.
- Getting background information on the people involved.
- Doing Internet or library research to confirm facts or claims.
- Determining the true costs and requirements you'll encounter.
- Checking references.

It's all about using research to *minimize* the unknowns. You're simply "doing your homework."

**Simply stated, POSEMs are about
"doing your homework."**

ACTION POSEMs

The way you pursue the opportunity you've identified will influence your chances of success. Action POSEMs include—

- Drawing on the experience of a friend or colleague as you proceed.
- Seeking a mentor who has experience that will benefit you.

- Retaining a career or performance coach to provide added perspective and assist you with refining your plan and improving your execution.

- Retaining a consultant experienced in the field of the opportunity to advise you.

- For a business initiative, putting someone on your team who has successfully pursued a similar initiative.

- For a business start-up, purchasing a franchise that provides an established plan to follow.

- For a business venture, taking on a partner who brings a complementary skill set and/or background.

- For an extensive business venture, taking on investors or obtaining financing to have working capital available.

SWIMMING WITHOUT THE SHARKS

I met a fellow on a visit to Hawaii who did a fantastic job of maximizing his chances of a positive outcome through POSEMs. Here's his story:

Brad had lived in Maui for a few years and was really enjoying the setting, but felt frustrated that he wasn't taking advantage of his access to the ocean for swimming. He wanted to get into ocean swimming for the exercise, the cooling effect during hot weather, and the sheer joy of it.

But he was concerned about the dangers of ocean swimming off Maui and for good reason. According to the state of Hawaii, from 1990 through 2004, there were 16 shark attacks on humans in the waters off Maui, one of which was fatal.[13] Knowing this had kept Brad on shore. Finally, Brad's frustration drove him to do some research on what he could do to reduce the chances of being attacked by a shark.

Now, you might be saying, "I know the solution. Stay on shore!" And of course, you're right. By staying on shore, Brad would be certain not to become a shark's lunch. But that wasn't an acceptable solution for Brad, so he set about doing what all successful risk-takers do—minimize the possible negative outcomes of a risk instead of taking the easy, and much less rewarding, course of just not taking the risk at all.

> **Brad set about doing what all successful risk-takers do—minimize the possible negative outcomes of a risk instead of taking the easy, and much less rewarding, course of just not taking the risk at all.**

Remember, risk is a tool to be exploited for your advantage. Like any other tool, it has value only if it's used. The most innovative, sophisticated power tool is useless sitting in your toolbox.

> **Risk is a tool to be exploited for your advantage. Like any other tool, it has value only if it's used. The most innovative, sophisticated power tool is useless sitting in your toolbox.**

Brad did his research and then took actions based on what he learned. He learned that there are a number of things he could do to significantly reduce the chances of sharks attacking. Here are the five POSEMs Brad implemented.

1. Brad does not swim during limited light at dusk, dawn, or night when some sharks move toward the shore to feed.
2. He does not swim in river runoff because sharks are known to like frequenting these waters for scavenging.
3. He stays out of what he calls "shark pits," which he describes as deep, cold water more than 100 feet in depth which he assesses by the visibility of the ocean floor. If he can't see the bottom, he

is out of there and does not return. This POSEM is driven by Brad's observation that shallow water gets warmed by the sun and sharks prefer cooler water.

4. He does not swim when he has any open cuts or when he can see distressed animals such as sick seals or whales that may attract sharks.

5. He researched Maui's history of shark attacks to identify which beaches are most prone to attacks.

Brad also identified a POSEM he chose not to take. He decided not to swim with a shark-repelling pod due to its high cost and uncertain effectiveness.

This brings up an important point. As you identify POSEMs, keep in mind that you don't need to implement every one. Some may have undesirable negative impacts. Again, employ your hard-earned judgment in the risk-taking process.

As you identify POSEMs, keep in mind that you don't need to implement every one. Some may have undesirable negative impacts.

So what did Brad have to show for all his careful research and implementation of POSEMs? Today, he thoroughly enjoys his almost-daily swims, he finds the hot summer weather more tolerable, and he's lost 20 pounds from the exercise. Brad is taking disciplined risks and doing it well!

Continuing the example from the last chapter—the opportunity of pursuing a new position with your current employer—examine the following POSEMs.

EXAMPLE

POSEMs

Identify as many Possibility of Success Enhancement Measures (POSEMs) you can think of that will (1) increase the likelihood of desirable Outcomes, and (2) decrease the likelihood of undesirable Outcomes.

A. Talk with people who work for the person who would be your supervisor to find out if he or she is an effective leader.

_____

B. Talk with people who are in a similar position to find out what they like and dislike about the role.

_____

C. Get the opinion of others, higher in the organization, regarding whether they see taking the position as a good career move.

_____

D. Consider what positions will likely be available to you in the future if you perform effectively in this position and whether these opportunities interest you.

_____

E. Additional actions

_____

It's your turn to identify POSEMs for the opportunity you're considering.

POSEMs

Identify as many Possibility of Success Enhancement Measures (POSEMs) you can think of that will (1) increase the likelihood of desirable Outcomes, and (2) decrease the likelihood of undesirable Outcomes.

A.

_____

B.

_____

C.

_____

D.

_____

E.

_____

Step 7—Revise the Likelihoods

"Two roads diverge in a wood,
and I took the one less traveled by,
and that has made all the difference."
ROBERT FROST

The POSEMs you have identified and plan to implement have changed things. They have improved your chances of success in the opportunity you're considering. That requires revising the distribution of Likelihoods for your Possible Outcomes determined in the last chapter. With your new POSEMs in mind, update the Likelihoods you've assigned to each Possible Outcome.

Continuing our example of pursuing a new position with your current employer, we'd modify the Possible Outcomes Matrix in this way.

EXAMPLE

Step 7—Revise the Likelihoods

Possible Outcome		Outcome Number	Initial Likelihood	Improved Likelihood
Best Case	more rewarding position	# 1	~~30~~ %	**40** %
Intermediate	equally rewarding position	# 2	~~40~~ %	**45** %
Intermediate		# ___	___ %	___ %
Intermediate		# ___	___ %	___ %
Worst Case	less rewarding position	# 3	~~30~~ %	**15** %
			100 %	**100** %

Now it's your turn. Go back to your Possible Outcomes Matrix in the last chapter and revise the percentages you assigned to the Likelihoods based on your POSEMs.

Step 8—Update Your Outcome Graphic

If showing the distribution of Likelihoods on the Possible Outcomes Graphic in the last chapter was helpful, you'll want to update it with the new Likelihoods.

For our example, here's how the revised Possible Outcomes Graphic will look.

EXAMPLE

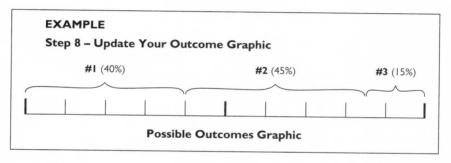

Things are looking better. The chances of a desirable outcome have increased and the chances of an undesirable outcome have decreased. This is progress.

It's your turn. Go ahead and create a new Possible Outcomes Graphic using your revised Likelihoods.

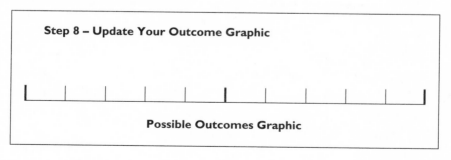

Step 9—Disaster Check

It's time to take a moment to assess what you have. Look at the Possible Outcomes you've identified. Are any of them *completely* unacceptable for you? If so, go no further. This means the opportunity doesn't make sense for you.

This may happen occasionally. There may be an outcome that, even though unlikely, is unacceptable. If that is the case and this process allows you to realize it, then the process has served you well. It is best to pass on *this* opportunity and move on to assessing another.

Hopefully, this is not the case and you can now move on to the final step.

Step 10—Decide

> *"Don't fear failure so much that you refuse to try new things. The saddest summary of a life contains three descriptions: could have, might have and should have."*
> LOUIS E. BOONE

We're at the last step. You've identified, assessed, and reassessed the opportunity. You've come up with actions you can take to positively affect the results of pursuing the opportunity. It's time to make your decision.

Are the chances of a desirable outcome high enough for the risks involved to make sense?

If you've not already decided, go back and look at your revised Possible Outcomes Matrix and Possible Outcomes Graphic. Dig deep. Are you ready to proceed? Are the chances of a desirable outcome high enough for the risks involved to make sense? Can you live with the Worst Case Outcome should it occur?

Keep in mind, you can—and should—come up with more POSEMs as you proceed. Doing so will further improve your chances for successful outcomes.

Remember, even with all your efforts, experiencing a Positive Outcome is likely but not certain. Consider the wisdom of Swiss poet and philosopher Henri Frédéric Amiel who lived in the 1800s:

> *"The man who insists upon seeing*
> *with perfect clearness before he decides,*
> *never decides."*
> HENRI FRÉDÉRIC AMIEL

You may find you'd like to pursue this opportunity, but you're experiencing some fear that is holding you back. That's all right. Chapter 9 addresses how to manage fear so you won't shrink from opportunities you'd like to pursue and risks you'd like to take.

Not Letting Fear Hold You Back

"Courage is very important. Like a
muscle, it is strengthened by use."
RUTH GORDON

Having gone to all the effort of analyzing an opportunity, thinking through possible outcomes and coming up with steps you can take to increase your chances of success, you may still be hesitant to proceed.

Fear is an ever-present part of pursuing
opportunities and taking risks.

In Chapter 4, it was mentioned that fear is an ever-present part of pursuing opportunities and taking risks. Next, we will discuss fear in an effort to do everything possible to keep it from limiting you.

THE BENEFIT OF FEAR

> *"Anything I've ever done that ultimately was worthwhile ... initially scared me to death."*
> BETTY BENDER

Fear is a gift to be welcomed. It tells you to stop, determine what's causing the fear, identify the insights it's providing, and adapt your plans accordingly.

Fear is a gift to be welcomed. To a point, it serves you well because it tells you something doesn't feel right. It also tells you to stop, determine what's causing the fear, identify the insights it's providing, and adapt your plans accordingly.

The problem occurs when you follow the fear response blindly, allow it to control you, and end up not taking action. That's when you're not learning from the fear but just letting it prevail over you.

The problem occurs when you follow the fear response blindly, allow it to control you, and end up not taking action. That's when you're not learning from the fear but just letting it prevail over you.

We are wired to respond to our fear impulses and give them priority over more rational thought. Research conducted by Joseph LeDoux, a professor of neuroscience at New York University, showed that the part of our brain that triggers the fight-or-flight response and pumps adrenaline into our bloodstream responds to a perceived threat faster than the parts of our brain that are more rational and capable of accurately assessing the validity of the threat.[14] That makes sense as a survival trait. But it's clearly something to be aware of so we don't let the initial fear response prevail when it doesn't serves us.

Since the visceral and emotional response to fear has a "priority" in our minds, we need to let it occur but make sure we do not let that be the end of it. To use an election-night example, all the votes aren't in. Think of the visceral response as simply the vote totals for the first few precincts. We must make sure we delay our decisions until receiving and considering the rest of the votes—that is, the more rational and intellectual responses.

PERCEIVED RISKS AND UNSUPPORTED FEARS

Perhaps the easiest fears to set aside are the ones not supported by fact. These are perceived risks that really are not risks at all. And they're found everywhere.

Every time a study comes out identifying a new potential danger, the media love to run with it. It makes sense. Every news producer wants something that challenges common beliefs because that's what makes news. Your challenge is to make sure you stay sufficiently well informed, that you know if the new "danger" is later proven to be unsupported. Should that happen, it doesn't tend to get the same media attention it got when it was first "discovered."

Take the example of the cancer risk of cell phones. How many times have you seen, read, or heard a news story telling you that cell phones can cause brain cancer? Likely, many times. I even know people who will only use a cell phone with a headset or ear piece because of their fear of cancer. I understand their concern. They have read or heard about the cancer threat of the phones many times.

As it turns out, this is one of many unsupported fears. A huge study that involved 420,000 cell phone users, some of whom had used cell phones for 21 years, showed no increased incidence of cancer compared with people who do not use cell phones. So, this is an unsupported fear. But unless you happen to have been reading the back pages of a newspaper when this study was issued, you are likely not aware of it and may still be carrying the belief that cell phones present a cancer risk.[15]

**There are likely to be many things
you see as risks that are not.**

This link between cancer and cell phone use is a perceived but unsupported risk. There are likely to be many things you see as risks that are not. They may be unsupported fears and not based in fact. Some simple research may help you set those fears aside.

Many fears are just not based in fact. Which of these activities do you think is most likely to result in your injury or death?

- swimming in the ocean
- snow skiing
- riding a bicycle on public streets
- flying on a commercial air taxi with fewer than ten seats
- snowboarding
- traveling in a car

You might be thinking, "This is a trick question." But it isn't. Looking at that list, most of us would assume that traveling in a car is easily the safest of the activities listed. And we would be absolutely wrong. It is the most likely to result in injury or death.[16]

**Do research to see if the fears you are
concerned about are even valid.**

Your intuitive response may have been wrong. What's the lesson to be learned? Not only to make sure you don't let fears control you, but to do research to see if the fears you're concerned about are even valid.

Here's another opportunity to possibly revise your perception of risk. While these issues have received a fair amount of attention in the media, guess how many people have died in the United States from bird flu and mad cow disease? As you consider your answer, keep in mind that the number is fewer than those who die each year in the U.S. from falling down stairs (1,588), choking on food (875), falling out of bed (594), slipping in ice or snow (103), anorexia (79), being stung by bees and wasps (66), being struck by lightning (47), skydiving (22), or contracting measles (1).[17]

How many people have died in the United States from bird flu and mad cow disease? As of this writing, exactly zero. Yet both risks receive a lot more attention than significant risks like falling down stairs or out of bed. Again, research the *actual* chances of a risk having a bad outcome versus the *perceived* chances.

There's something more to consider when you're experiencing fear. Two highly regarded researchers at the Harvard Center for Risk Analysis, David Ropeik and George Gray, Ph.D., offer a thought-provoking insight in their book *Risk—A Practical Guide for Deciding What's Really Safe and What's Really Dangerous in the World Around You.* Consider this:

> The psychology of risk perception has found that we tend to be more afraid of something if it is man-made and less afraid if it's natural.

> There are several types of radiation-related hazards that evoke deep public concern, all of which are man-made: nuclear power, cell phones, X-rays. But far and away the most significant radiation-related risk to human health is natural (solar radiation), yet it gets a lot less attention and causes much less worry.[18]

Interesting. This means we tend to pay more attention to man-made sources of risk and less to naturally occurring ones. These are all factors to consider when liberating yourself from the immobilizing impact of fear.

We tend to be more afraid of something if it is man-made and less afraid if it occurs naturally.

Think of it like this: You're experiencing fear about a trip to a place you've never visited. Your goal is to make that fear a *roadmap* and not a *roadblock*. When you learn from what the fear is telling you, it helps you navigate and make the trip successful. If the fear causes you to cancel the trip and stay home, you're allowing the fear to be a roadblock. Fear wins. You lose.

The goal is to make fear a roadmap and not a roadblock.

THE FIRST CRITICAL STEP

"Face adversity promptly and without flinching, and you will reduce its impact."
WINSTON CHURCHILL

What is the first step in benefiting from fear instead of falling victim to it? Acknowledging it. Yes, as simple as it sounds, this is a critical first step that many people don't take.

When you acknowledge any fear you're experiencing, its mystery and a great deal of the power of the fear dissipates.

When you acknowledge and accept any fear you're experiencing, its mystery and, as a result, a great deal of the power of the fear dissipates. That puts you in a place to exploit it instead of being controlled by it.

The benefit of accepting fear when confronted with it is something I've learned in my skydiving career. Many times, I've been confronted with potentially immobilizing fears, most often before a particularly challenging exhibition skydive.

Exhibition skydives into public events can be extra challenging with their small landing area, obstructions such as power lines and light poles, limited or no alternative landing areas, less than ideal conditions such as high or variable winds and cloud cover or a combination of these challenges.

These potentially life-threatening situations are a particularly bad time to fall victim to impaired judgment caused by fear. As a skydiver, at a time like this I need to be able to make assessments and decisions unclouded by fear.

Early on, I learned from a highly experienced exhibition skydiver that trying to deny the fear or hide it from others doesn't work. He spoke openly of being afraid before these skydives. His honesty allowed me to escape my self-deception and acknowledge my fear. It works.

Once you have accepted the fear that a situation presents, you can move forward to make better decisions that yield better outcomes.

Once I have accepted the nearly inevitable fear in one of these situations, I can move forward to make better decisions that yield better outcomes.

I've long said that one of the most important skills needed to be a successful exhibition skydiver is knowing when to stay in the plane. This may sound odd. And if you find skydiving innately absurd, you might be thinking, "You should *always* stay in the plane!"

I can understand that sentiment. While I'm comfortable with the risks of skydiving, there are plenty of risks I consider unjustified. One example is visiting parts of the world where you run a serious risk of contracting in incurable disease. While I don't fault people who do so, I find that an unacceptable risk.

But, back to exhibition skydives. Most problems related to exhibition skydives have nothing to do with a lack of ability. Rather, they almost always can be traced to insufficient planning, poor decision-making, or both.

Putting a bunch of skydivers in a plane and giving them a landing area ringed by a large crowd and television cameras sets up a volatile situation. Experienced skydivers are innately confident and, at times, overconfident. By the time we're about to jump, adrenaline is coursing through our veins.

All these factors make it hard to decide to stay in the plane and abort the skydive, *even when conditions dictate that we should.* Add to that the fact that staying in the plane can result in reduced or no compensation for the jump. And equally bad, fellow jumpers not present rarely hesitate to second guess your decision after the fact.

Yet knowing when to stay in the plane is part of going from being an exhibition skydiver to being a *professional* exhibition skydiver. The pros know how to manage the situation and their fears in such high-stress environments.

You can easily see why an exhibition skydiver's judgment at the moment of decision can be less than perfect. To this precarious mixture, if you add flawed judgment due to unacknowledged fear, you have a good chance for a bad outcome. As you can see, acknowledging and accepting fear in this situation to minimize its effect is vital.

Doing so has served me well. I have successfully completed hundreds of exhibition skydives without injuries to members of the audience, other jumpers, or myself. I've had to land in alternate landing areas a few times, resulting in a seriously bruised ego. Other times, I made the choice to stay in the plane, but that's what it takes sometimes. I know people who've lost their lives by making bad decisions on an exhibition skydive. It's a serious business.

> *"Courage is resistance to fear, mastery*
> *of fear, not absence of fear."*
> MARK TWAIN

A HIGH DIVING EXAMPLE

One of my fellow risk-takers is Bill Treasurer. Bill spent many years on the U.S. High Diving Team. High diving is not for the faint of heart. High divers start with 100-foot dives and go up from there (compared with Olympic divers whose highest jumps are from only 33 feet.

High divers can achieve speeds of almost 50 miles per hour before hitting the water, their only protective gear being a mouthpiece. Clearly, to be successful in this realm, you must have effective fear management techniques.

As you'd expect, Bill has developed some interesting insights on managing fear. He learned in his high diving days that fear needs to be respected. He presents fear as having the ability to empower you. As Bill puts it, "High divers aren't fearless, they are fear-enhanced. It is precisely this fear that heightens divers' awareness of their surroundings so they won't make mistakes."[19] His basic concept is that fear can lead to respect for the challenge, which can then lead to a successful outcome.

I agree with Bill and would add that a constructive manifestation of fear is showing respect for it by thoughtfully devising and implementing POSEMs, as discussed in the last chapter.

FURTHER VALIDATION FOR ACKNOWLEDGING FEAR

The power of acknowledging fear when it surfaces has been validated by empirical research.

Early in the space program, the National Aeronautics and Space Administration (NASA) observed that some astronauts could complete their missions without showing physical manifestations of motion and anxiety sickness, yet others did. Interestingly, there was no crossover between the two groups—either they were having the problem or they weren't.

The astronauts completing their mission without getting sick where the ones who were acknowledging in advance, to themselves and possibly others, that they were going to experience fear.

Because the situation could affect an astronaut's performance, NASA commissioned research to determine the cause of the condition. The results revealed only one factor that differentiated the two groups.

- The astronauts getting ill were the ones who were not consciously acknowledging the fear that would be a part of their missions.
- The astronauts completing their mission without getting sick where the ones who were acknowledging in advance, to themselves (and possibly others), that they were going to experience fear.

Their willingness to acknowledge the fear they would understandably experience was the difference. It spared them a physical response and made them more effective. This illustrates how profound it is to acknowledge the fear we experience at various times.

Back on earth, I was contacted by Mick, an audience member who had heard my message encouraging him to accept his fears. In Mick's case, the impact of fear was profound. He had battled a severe stutter all his life. Nothing he had tried over his 40-year life span had helped him get past this career-limiting challenge.

A few months after he heard my presentation, Mick contacted me. He told me that he had implemented the steps I suggested in my presentation, starting with accepting the presence of the fears he was experiencing. His results amazed everyone. In a later email, he told me he actually delivered a one-hour speech at a conference for speech pathologists without stuttering once!

Accepting that fear will likely be present when you take risks is a constructive critical step that will serve you well and reduce much of the negative impact of the fear.

I hope I've convinced you by now that accepting that fear will likely be present when you take risks is a constructive critical step that will serve you well and reduce much of the negative impact of the fear. So bask in it! You may be somewhat, or even significantly, afraid. That's all right.

DISSECTING THE FEAR

"Confront your fears, list them, get to know them,
and only then will you be able to put
them aside and move ahead."
JERRY GILLIES

In Chapter 4, I mentioned that fears come in two forms, Emotional and Mental. Emotional Fears are gut driven and visceral. Mental Fears are mind driven and rational. Research by Paul Slovic, professor of psychology at the

University of Oregon, supports this assessment. Professor Slovic concluded that we have an automatic, intuitive system and a more thoughtful, analytical system for analyzing risk. He states that our perception of risk lives largely in our feelings, so most of the time we are operating in the automatic, intuitive system.[20] Slovic's automatic, intuitive system is what I refer to as Emotional Fear. His thoughtful, analytical system is the Mental Fear.

Let's dig further into this differentiation. The goal is to minimize Emotional Fear and learn from Mental Fear. Remember this graphic?

The Fears

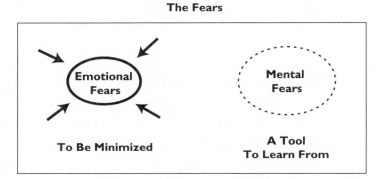

To start, how can you tell one from the other? Simply stated, you want to subject the fears you're experiencing as you prepare to pursue an opportunity to a *Reality Check*.

> *"Half our fears are baseless and the*
> *other half discreditable."*
> CHRISTIAN NESTELL BOVEE

REALITY CHECK

The first step in subjecting your fears to a Reality Check is to identify them. Pull out a blank sheet of paper and start listing them. It doesn't matter how baseless or foolish they may seem, write them down on paper.

Not only will this exercise facilitate the Reality Check, it will start to expose your fears to the light of day. Until they're identified and acknowledged, they swirl around in the recesses of your mind confusing and intimidating you. Yet once they're on a piece of paper, something powerful happens. They lose some of their hold over you. They seem much less frightening when they're reduced to a few words on paper than when they're playing hide and seek in your mind. You may even find fewer exist than you expected.

An Example of a Reality Check

The fears I subject to the Reality Check are those I may experience when confronted with a particularly challenging exhibition skydive. Lots of things can go wrong when performing an exhibition skydive; some can even cause the event to flop and others can result in injuries or death.

Here's what I list when I ask myself what fears I experience putting together an exhibition skydive.

EXAMPLE

Step 1 of the Reality Check—List the Fears
Fears
1. Forgetting some gear
2. Arriving at the wrong place
3. Ground crew not showing up
4. Aircraft not arriving at assigned time and location
5. Aircraft malfunction
6. Equipment malfunction
7. Pilot error
8. Not being able to find the target
9. Air traffic control problems
10. Ground crew mistakes

11. Miscommunication resulting in a flawed performance
12. Dissatisfied client
13. Unsafe weather conditions
14. Injury or death of a jumper
15. Injury or death of a spectator
16. A devastating earthquake making the landing area unsafe after we exit the jump plane

LIST YOUR CONCERNS AND FEARS

It is your turn. Take an opportunity you are considering and write down the concerns and fears it raises. With your fears listed on paper and a little less intimidating, the next step is to take an objective look at each one and label it valid or invalid.

DETERMINE WHETHER FEARS ARE VALID OR INVALID

In my example, I listed at least one fear that's invalid on its face—that is, an Emotional Fear about the earthquake. That's crazy. I put it there to make a point: While there's an *infinitesimal* chance of an earthquake occurring, the possibility is so slight that it's absurd to worry about it. A meteorite could also impact the landing area moments before we land! As crazy as it sounds, some people do let such highly unlikely possibilities concern them. Don't be one of them.

So as your next step, label as invalid any fears that just do not justify your concern.

At first glance, the rest of the fears I have listed seem valid, but many are not—even though they are rational fears based on sound reasoning and hence Mental Fears. They are not valid because I will implement numerous POSEMs—Possibility of Success Enhancement Measures—to make their occurrence extremely unlikely just as you learned to do in the last chapter.

In the absence of POSEMs such as extensive preparation and continual practice, many of these fears would be justified and, hence, valid. POSEMs such as systems and checklists developed over many years significantly reduce the chances of negative outcomes. This makes many of these fears either invalid or valid but highly unlikely, hence effectively invalid.

To be brief, I won't list all the POSEMs I would implement. You don't need them identified to understand the point and how it applies to you. Just know that most of them involve verifying arrangements, double-checking equipment, and managing expectations. Just be assured that many POSEMs render most of these fears invalid.

So, this is how my list of fears and concerns now looks.

EXAMPLE

Step 2 of the Reality Check—Determine Validity

Fear	Valid	Invalid
1. Forgetting some gear		X
2. Arriving at the wrong place		X
3. Ground crew not showing up		X
4. Aircraft not arriving at assigned time and location		X
5. Aircraft malfunction	X	
6. Equipment malfunction	X	
7. Pilot error	X	
8. Not being able to find the target		X
9. Air traffic control problems	X	
10. Ground crew mistakes		X
11. Miscommunication resulting in a flawed performance		X
12. Dissatisfied client		X

13. Unsafe weather conditions	X	
14. Injury or death of a jumper		X
15. Injury or death of a spectator		X
16. A devastating earthquake affecting the landing area after we exit the plane		X

Now that you've identified the fears listed as either valid or invalid, the next step is to learn from the *valid* fears.

LEARN FROM YOUR VALID FEARS

Looking at the fears you've determined to be valid, ask what you can learn from each of them. What insights are they giving you? What do they suggest you should be doing differently? Or is there nothing you can do to address them but acknowledge they exist and not let them control you?

Here's that process using our ongoing example.

EXAMPLE

Step 3 of the Reality Check—Learning from the Valid Fears

In this example, five valid fears were identified. They are:

1. aircraft malfunction
2. equipment malfunction
3. pilot error
4. air traffic control problems
5. unsafe weather conditions

What can I learn from them?

Aircraft Malfunction—While I've never had an aircraft malfunction on an exhibition skydive, it is always a possibility. I can't totally eliminate the chances of it happening. What I can do is perhaps be more careful in selecting aircraft. In the past, I've been inclined to use a plane that's either stationed closest to the jump location or operated by someone I know.

I have not thought about which aircraft is newest or best maintained. My insight from this fear is that I should include these factors when I select a plane to use for an exhibition jump. This means I may have to incur an extra expense to have the aircraft brought in from a greater distance in the interest of reducing the chances of an aircraft malfunction.

If the aircraft is coming from far enough away, I may also have to incur the cost of paying for the pilot to fly in the day before and stay overnight near the airport. In both cases, I may need to incur extra expenses to reduce the chances of a problem.

As you can see, identifying and seeking insights from this Valid Fear has served me well.

As I look at the other valid fears listed, I recognize things I can learn.

See the idea? Now delve into the valid fears on your list and see what you can learn from them.

> **By going through the process of identifying your fears and concerns, you will not only find you are dealing with fewer fears, but they will have less impact on you. They may also provide you with valuable insights.**

By going through the process of identifying the fears and concerns you are experiencing as you prepare to take a risk and then determining their validity, you will not only find you're dealing with fewer fears, but they will have less impact on you. They may also provide you with valuable insights.

BE ATTENTIVE TO YOUR INTUITION

An important part of being good at taking risks and seizing opportunities is paying attention to your intuition—a vital part of being a successful risk-taker. You ignore your intuition at your peril.

**An important part of being good at
taking risks and seizing opportunities is
paying attention to your intuition.**

Your intuition is a powerful tool that sends you insights regularly. If you don't do it already, I encourage you to listen carefully to it. I think of it like a radio signal that's always broadcasting. But a radio station does nothing for you if you don't turn on the radio and tune it to the right frequency. The most effective risk-takers keep the radio on and tuned to the right station.

Your intuition is a vital internal resource that will serve you well. Again, pay attention to it. No doubt you've heard stories of people who did or did not take an action because something inside told them to proceed or not proceed. They were being attentive to their intuition.

**I am suggesting that you be attentive to the voice
you have inside but sometimes forget to listen to.**

I'm not suggesting you sit in a lotus position on top of a rock and await divine guidance. Or that you cast chicken bones, read tea leaves, or abide by other superstitions. But I am suggesting you be attentive to the voice you have inside but sometimes forget to listen to.

This concept, as old as ancient history, was eloquently expressed by the person many consider the wisest man to have ever lived—King Solomon. In 950 B.C., he wrote:

*"Good advice lies deep within a person's
heart, the wise will draw it out."*
SOLOMON

DRAW ON LESSONS FROM PAST NEGATIVE OUTCOMES

Another source of valuable guidance is available to you. It's the lessons you can learn from past negative outcomes. You have of course taken risks that did not work out. There are insights awaiting you if you go back and assess these situations. Don't deprive yourself of these lessons!

> **You've taken risks that did not work out. There are insights awaiting you if you go back and assess these situations. Don't deprive yourself of these lessons!**

Please, don't make the mistake of deciding that one negative outcome when pursuing a certain outcome means you should never try something similar again. That's a seriously bad idea and a sure path to missed opportunities.

> **Don't make the mistake of deciding that one negative outcome means you should never try again.**

> *"He who has never failed somewhere...*
> *that man can not be great."*
> HERMAN MELVILLE

> **I'm not encouraging you pursue the same opportunity time and again without changing your approach when it has never resulted in success.**

I'm not encouraging you pursue the same opportunity time and again without changing your approach when it has never resulted in success. That makes no sense. But I *am* encouraging you to revisit the situation, think through why you didn't succeed, and identify what you could do differently next time to increase your chances of success. Very likely, there are POSEMs you can implement you didn't use last time.

Equally as important, don't just look for ideas of what to do better. Also look for the insights you can gain from a past unsuccessful experience. Ask these questions:

- Were the talents needed to succeed at odds with your Natural Skill Set?
- Did you make some ill-considered decisions you could have avoided with more thoughtful consideration?
- Would a few Research or Action POSEMs have resulted in a positive outcome?
- Did you seek advice from the wrong people?
- Did you ignore your intuition?
- What can you learn from that negative outcome?

There are insights from your answers awaiting you. You just need to invest time and thought to uncover them.

There are insights from your answers awaiting you. You just need to invest time and thought to uncover them.

INSIGHT FROM A NEGATIVE OUTCOME

One negative outcome during an exhibition skydive became a source of insight for me.

I was preparing to jump as part of an air show. As exhibition skydives go, this one was about as easy as they get since the landing area was a large airport. While there was a specific target, I had hundreds of acres I could land in if need be. Being an airport, there were no physical obstructions such as towers, poles, or buildings near the target. In addition, I'd be doing a practice jump hours in advance of the show so there would be no crowd at the time. This would be a piece of cake, or so I thought.

If the huge, clear landing area was not enough to give me a sense of false confidence, my last jump before this practice jump had been a treacherous, but successful, jump into Candlestick Park on the shore of persistently windy San Francisco Bay. After succeeding at one of the most challenging jumps ever, my confidence was riding high. I thought I was close to walking on water.

Well, I quickly learned that, instead of walking on water, I had feet of stone.

Feeling invincible for that practice jump, I wasn't as focused as I needed to be. I initiated my landing flair too late. If I'd timed it correctly, it would have set me down on the taxiway lightly. Instead, I had a painfully hard landing and a severely sprained ankle. And I mean severely sprained. Within minutes, my entire foot turned different shades of purple and I was in serious agony. I had a pronounced limp for long time as I recovered from this—the worst skydiving injury I've ever experienced.

What was my lesson? Not to be overconfident and deceive myself into thinking I'm invincible. It doesn't matter how seemingly simple a jump is or how well a recent one went. Each one presents its own opportunity for big problems. I need to respect each jump and give it my full and focused attention.

Past negative outcomes don't need to hold you back. They are a gift from which to learn.

Remember, past negative outcomes don't need to hold you back. Treat them as a gift from which to learn. You just need to unwrap the gift.

"It is better to err on the side of daring
than the side of caution."
ALVIN TOFFLER

CHAPTER 10

Enjoying the Rewards of Risk-Taking

*"Courageous risks are life-giving, they help you grow,
make you brave, and better than you think you are."*

JOAN L. CURCIO

Why take risks? Why seize opportunities? Why put forth extra effort? Why challenge yourself? Why leave your Comfort Zone?

The answer to all these questions is the same—for the rewards you'll enjoy when you do.

When you take risks effectively, you'll experience rewards you otherwise would never enjoy. That's the driving force behind writing this book. *I want you to take risks successfully and wallow in the rewards you will earn by doing so.*

> **Applying these concepts will expand your horizons, add excitement and vitality to your life, bring new people into your world, and make life more fun.**

Not only will persistently applying the concepts in this book yield you rewards, it will expand your horizons, add excitement and vitality to your life, bring new people into your world, and make life more fun. When you challenge yourself to thoughtfully pursue opportunities, you'll enjoy rewards you otherwise would never experience. It comes down this statement I wrote:

> *A consistent pattern of intelligent risk-taking will*
> *yield rewards you otherwise would never experience.*
> JIM McCORMICK

In all the years I have been asserting this statement, no one has taken issue with it. I don't think you can. It's irrefutable.

There are some important qualifiers in that statement. They are *consistent* and *intelligent*. To enjoy the ongoing rewards of taking risks, you need to take them *consistently*. Taking them only occasionally won't do it. Risk-taking needs to be ongoing.

And the risks need to be taken *intelligently*. That's the whole point. I want to inspire you to take risks and be successful because you do it in an intelligent manner, thoughtfully and methodically, as this book shows you to do.

COMPOUND REWARDS

The rewards you'll enjoy as a direct result of taking intelligent risks come in two forms: *Direct Rewards* and *Compound Rewards*.

Direct Rewards are the rewards you can anticipate when considering a risk. And because they are known, they will be the basis for your decision whether to proceed.

Compound Rewards are the rewards you can't anticipate.

Compound Rewards are the rewards you can't anticipate when thinking about taking a risk and pursuing an opportunity. They are the surprises. Even though they are unknown at the time you are considering the risk, don't discount them. Compound Rewards could well turn out to be much more significant than the Direct Rewards.

Compound Rewards could well turn out to be much more significant than the Direct Rewards.

The best example from my own experiences is my deciding to be a member of the skydiving expedition to the North Pole and then taking the risk of leaving the jump plane in the middle of the Arctic.

In retrospect, the Direct Rewards I could anticipate were minor compared to the Compound Rewards I have enjoyed. Over the top of the Polar Cap, looking out the plane and having just addressed some potentially serious gear problems, I could only identify three Direct Rewards I would enjoy if I proceeded out of the door and went into freefall.

1. I would experience freefall over the Polar Cap.
2. I would make it to the North Pole.
3. And I would make it back home.

These were the only reasons I could come up with to leave that four-engine jet and make the jump. I had no way of knowing the Compound Rewards at that moment—that it would be a Turning Point in my life that would ultimately take my career in a whole new direction.

That experience was the first of many that has lead people to see me as an expert on intelligent risk-taking. It has allowed me to achieve a lifelong dream of working for myself by providing coaching, consulting, workshops, motivational presentations, and now writing this book. All these are Compound Rewards I can track directly to the risk of skydiving to the North Pole. As you can see, with time, the Compound Rewards have far outweighed the Direct Rewards of this extraordinary jump.

That is how it will work for you. When you are willing to—

- challenge yourself,
- assess your Personal Risk Inclination,
- determine and respect your Natural Skill Set,
- exploit your strengths,
- bolster your weaknesses,
- identify opportunities and likely outcomes,
- determine and implement POSEMs,
- manage your fear, and
- proceed both boldly and thoughtfully.

Opportunities will appear to you that you'd otherwise never discover.

Not only will doors of opportunity open that would otherwise remain closed, but many will appear to you that you'd otherwise never discover.

Think of it like this: You're standing at the end of a long hallway with many doors on either side, like standing in the hallway of a large hotel. Each door represents an opportunity available to you as you proceed down the corridor of life.

When you take the steps laid out in this book and summarized above, not only will some of the doors open to you as you proceed down the hallway, but you'll realize there are many more doors than you could see at first. These additional doors lead to the Compound Rewards that will come your way because you were willing to risk.

THE DECISION IS YOURS

Only you can make the decision to proceed.

It all starts with your decision to proceed—a decision only *you* can make. There are plenty of people and resources to help you pursue opportunities successfully. And once you decide to proceed, they all become available to you.

I desperately hope you will make the decision to move forward. Great joy, excitement, vitality, and expanded horizons await you when you do. Always remember—

> *The greatest rewards in life*
> *go to the risk-takers.*
> JIM MCCORMICK

The decision is yours.

About the Author

Author Jim McCormick approaches writing the same way he earned an MBA; taught executive level management courses; served a Presidential administration; parachuted to the North Pole; captured five skydiving world records; performed as an executive for successful real estate and architectural companies; and has spoken before thousands of people seeking inspiration and direction in their professional and personal lives—one carefully calculated risk at a time. Jim's skydiving and speaking adventures can be explored at *TakeRisks.com*.

Appendix

RESEARCH RESULTS

The research on risk inclination addressed in Chapter 2 yielded many interesting insights. They are detailed in this appendix.

Averages and Ranges of Assessments—On average, people placed their risk inclination for all types of risks between 5.4 and 7.6. It's interesting that the averages are all above the midpoint on the assessment scale. It's also noteworthy that the range is relatively small with only 2.2 points between the lower and higher averages. This suggests that people, as a whole, consider themselves moderately risk inclined and see their risk inclination in all areas as reasonably similar.

Individually, the range of risk inclination for the specific risks varied the maximum possible—that is, people assessed their risk inclinations all the way from 1 to 10.

The averages of all risks for men varied from 5.9 to 7.5, a range of 1.6. The average risk inclinations for all risks for women had a notably broader range of 2.7, ranging from 4.9 to 7.6.

Highest Assessment—Both as a whole and when broken down by gender, survey respondents indicated they were most comfortable taking intellectual risks. This could be due to people seeing the downside of intellectual risks as more acceptable than negative outcomes from financial, relationship, or physical risks. Put another way, because intellectual risks are private in nature, they're usually taken without anyone being aware of the risk except the person taking it. As such, if a negative outcome occurs, it's likely known only to the risk-taker.

Survey respondents indicated they were most comfortable taking intellectual risks.

Lowest Assessment—Overall, people identified physical and financial risks as the ones they were least comfortable taking. With the average age of the respondents being in the late 40s, age likely influenced this outcome. This result was consistent for both men and women. Men assessed their risk inclination in financial risks as their lowest, with physical risk inclination almost the same. Women identified physical risks as the ones they were least inclined to take, with financial risks a close second.

People identified physical and financial risks as the ones they were least inclined to take.

Gender Differences—It's interesting to note in which areas men's and women's average risk inclination is the same. They see their inclination to take social, intellectual, creative, and relationship risks as identical. The area with the greatest difference in perceived risk inclination between men and women isn't surprising. It occurs in physical risks. On average, men indicated that their inclination to take physical risks is 6.0. For women, it is 4.9. This range of 1.1 is the largest difference in risk inclination that occurs when comparing results by gender. The second largest variance in risk inclination by gender is for financial risks with the averages for males at 5.9 and females at 5.1.

The area with the greatest difference in risk inclination between men and women is physical risks.

There is only one type of risk for which women indicated a greater risk inclination than men—that is, spiritual risks. It is surprising to note that men self-assessed their risk inclination in emotional risks higher than women.

Revised Overall Risk Inclination—One point of this exercise is to encourage people to look at their risk inclination more broadly. That's the reason respondents are asked to assess their Overall Risk Inclination again *after* assessing their inclination to take risks in nine specific areas. Many respondents revised their Overall Risk Inclination as a result of completing the survey.

- Almost half of the people completing the profile moved their general risk inclination upward (toward more risk inclined) the second time they assessed their Overall Risk Inclination compared to their first response. That means that simply looking at their risk profile more broadly allowed them to revise their Overall Risk Inclination upward—a powerful result.
- For women, this effect was even more dramatic than for men. Over half of the women taking the survey increased their Overall Risk Inclination while two in five men did the same.
- One-third of those taking the survey did not change their Overall Risk Inclination, with the results for men and women not much different.

- Some people revised their Overall Risk Inclination downward as a result of taking the survey, but fewer than one in five.

- For every person who moved their final Overall Risk Inclination downward compared to their initial Overall Risk Inclination, almost three moved theirs upward.

- For women, only 14 percent moved their assessments downward, while 23 percent of men did the same.

To review, almost half of the respondents moved their assessments of their Overall Risk Inclination upward. A little more than one-third kept theirs the same and fewer than one in five moved theirs downward.

After looking more broadly at their risk inclination, almost half moved their assessments of their Overall Risk Inclination upward. A little more than one-third kept theirs the same and fewer than one in five moved theirs downward.

Breadth of Responses—It is interesting to look at which risk areas had the narrowest distribution of assessments and which ones were the broadest. (The standard deviation of the responses presented in the data indicates this breadth.)

The narrowest response distribution indicates that, overall, the risk inclination for that specific risk was the most similar among those taking the survey. Intellectual and relationship risks had the narrowest distribution of responses indicating the most similar responses. Men showed the least variance in intellectual and financial risk inclination. For women, relationship risks followed by financial and career risks showed the narrowest range of responses. This means that these are the types of risks where any given respondent, on average, sees themselves as most similar to all the others completing the survey.

Independent of gender, spiritual risks showed the greatest variance in responses, followed closely by physical risks. While tallying the responses, we noticed that it was common for the assessment of spiritual risks to vary significantly from all of a person's other assessments. This broad range of assessments of spiritual risk inclination is interesting and seems to support the notable divide in American society between those who have a religious orientation and those who see the world in more secular terms.

Spiritual risks showed the greatest variance in responses.

More Influential Risk Inclinations—I have long suspected that we allow our comfort level with certain kinds of risks to disproportionately influence our perception of our Overall Risk Inclination. A goal of this survey is to look for a correlation between the first assessment of Overall Risk Inclination and risk inclination in the various specific areas that would provide evidence of such disproportionate influence.

Based on many conversations, I've sensed that many people allow their comfort level with physical risks to significantly and perhaps disproportionately influence their perception of their Overall Risk Inclination. But I have been wary to assert this due to the fact that most of the people who have indicated this to me are aware of my own willingness to take physical risks such as skydiving.

So how much correlation did we find between the respondents' first assessment of their Overall Risk Inclination and their physical risk inclination? It depends on what group of respondents you are looking at. For males, there was significant correlation between their initial Overall Risk Inclination with physical and financial risks.

For females, there was less correlation than for males, so the same theory does not seem valid. For women, the highest degree of correlation with the initial assessment of Overall Risk Inclination was with financial risks. None of the other eight risk categories showed significant correlation.

Impact of Age—I'm often asked how risk inclination changes with age. Research has shown that most people become more change adverse as they get older. But feeling comfortable with change is only part of the risk equation.

Trend analysis shows a reduction in risk inclination with age as would seem likely. While each person is unique in his or her risk inclination and how it changes with age, in the aggregate, the drop in risk inclination isn't that dramatic. This seems like a reasonably intuitive conclusion and not particularly surprising.

The research results show that those in their 70s have aggregate RQs that are only about 13.5 percent lower than respondents in their 20s. As with some of the other data, the results are more interesting when we look at the data by gender. The drop for women is significantly less than for men. For the same age ranges, women's aggregate RQs drop just over 12 percent while men's RQs drop over 16 percent. The higher drop for men is caused by their aggregate RQs starting higher when in their 20s.

The results get even more interesting when we look at average risk inclination broken down into ten-year age bands (20 to 29 years, 30 to 39 years, and so on). With both genders combined, risk inclination is fairly constant until the 60s. Then it drops off in the 70s and increases some-what from the 50s to the 60s. This could suggest an increase in willingness to take risks around retirement age before risk inclination drops. That's when the ravages of age start to take a heavy toll and one's income-earning potential drops. This increase in the 50s and 60s could also be influenced by increased financial security compared to earlier ages.

Looking only at men, we see a small but consistent drop in risk inclination with each decade until their 60s. As with the results for both genders, we see an increase in their 60s before a significant drop in their 70s.

Women show increased risk inclination from their 40s to their 50s and on into their 60s.

Looking at these same age-group averages for women shows increased risk inclination from their 40s to their 50s and on into their 60s. This could be related to increased personal and professional options after the obligations to raise a family have been fulfilled. Some sociologists have suggested that women spend the first half of their lives tending to the needs of others, then, in some cases, spend the second half of their lives addressing more of their own needs. That concept could be showing up in the survey results.

Details of Risk Inclination Research

Survey Population

	Males and Females		Males		Females	
Count	321	100%	132	41.1%	189	58.9%

Age Distribution Respondents

	Males and Females		Males		Females	
Age Range	21–75	54 yrs.	21–75	54 yrs.	21–75	54 yrs.

Changes in Self-Assessment of Overall Risk Inclination
After Assessing Risk Inclination for Nine Specific Types of Risks

	Males and Females	Males	Females
Increase from Initial to Second Overall Risk Inclination Assessment	48.3%	40.9%	53.4%
No Change from Initial to Second Overall Risk Inclination Assessment	34.0%	36.4%	32.3%
Decrease from Initial to Second Overall Risk Inclination Assessment	17.8%	22.7%	14.3%

Variance Between Initial Self-Assessment of Overall
Risk Inclination and Risk Quotient (RQ)

Derived by Averaging Self-Assessed Risk Inclination for
Nine Specific Types of Risks

	Males and Females	Males	Females
RQ Higher than Initial Assessment of Overall Risk Inclination	54.8%	45.5%	61.4%
RQ Effectively the Same as Initial Assessment of Overall Risk Inclination (variance of ± 0.5)	27.1%	27.3%	27.0%
RQ Lower than Initial Assessment of Overall Risk Inclination	18.1%	27.3%	11.6%

Variance Between Second Self-Assessment of Overall
Risk Inclination and Risk Quotient (RQ)

Derived by Averaging Self-Assessed Risk Inclination for
Nine Specific Types of Risks

	Males and Females	Males	Females
RQ Higher than Second Assessment of Overall Risk Inclination	33.6%	31.8%	35.1%
RQ Effectively the Same as Second Assessment of Overall Risk Inclination (variance of ±0.5)	47.7%	45.5%	49.5%
RQ Lower than Second Assessment of Overall Risk Inclination	18.7%	22.7%	15.4%

Significant Variances Between Second Self-Assessment of Overall Risk Inclination and Risk Quotient (RQ)

Derived by Averaging Self-Assessed Risk Inclination for Nine Specific Types of Risks

	Males and Females	Males	Females
RQ More than 2.0 Higher than Second Assessment of Overall Risk Inclination	3.1%	1.5%	6.1%
RQ More than 1.5 Higher than Second Assessment of Overall Risk Inclination	8.1%	4.5%	15.2%
RQ More than 1.5 Lower than Second Assessment of Overall Risk Inclination	1.6%	2.3%	1.5%
RQ More than 2.0 Lower than Second Assessment of Overall Risk Inclination	0.6%	0.8%	0.8%

Averages and Standard Deviations of Assessments and Ages

	Males and Females		Males		Females	
	Average	Standard Deviation	Average	Standard Deviation	Average	Standard Deviation
Initial Overall Risk Inclination	6.0	1.8	6.2	1.8	5.7	1.7
Physical Risks	5.5	2.4	6.0	2.5	5.0	2.3
Career Risks	6.7	2.0	6.8	2.1	6.5	2.1
Financial Risks	5.6	2.0	5.9	1.9	5.2	2.0
Social Risks	7.0	2.3	7.0	2.2	7.0	2.3
Intellectual Risks	7.5	2.0	7.5	1.9	7.5	2.1
Creative Risks	7.0	2.2	7.1	2.2	7.0	2.3
Relationship Risks	6.7	1.9	6.7	2.0	6.6	1.9
Emotional Risks	6.1	2.2	6.4	2.2	5.9	2.2
Spiritual Risks	6.5	2.6	6.5	2.7	6.6	2.5
Risk Quotient	6.5	1.3	6.7	1.3	6.4	1.3
Second Overall Risk Inclination	6.4	1.4	6.5	1.4	6.3	1.5
Age	48.1	12.2	48.4	11.6	48.0	12.7

Note: These trend analysis observations of the effects of age on risk inclination were derived by observing the slope of a least squares fit of the aggregate RQs plotted against the age of the corresponding respondent.

Glossary

Action POSEMs—Actions that increase the chances of a risk yielding a positive outcome and decrease the chances of a negative outcome. (See POSEMs.)

Actual Risk—The true level of risk with risk mitigation and success enhancement measures taken into account. The same risk without proposed risk mitigation and success enhancement actions taken into account is the Perceived Risk.

Areas for Improvement—One of three categories into which a person's capabilities are sorted in determining their Natural Skill Set. Areas for Improvement are the tasks and skills for which both ability and fulfillment are low. The other two categories are Strengths and Serviceable Skills. (Also see Weaknesses.)

Avoided Risk—A risk a person has determined to be unnecessary or undesirable for their normal functioning. Avoided Risks are not fixed and vary with time.

Best Case Outcome—The most desirable outcome that can result from a course of action.

Calling—The role to which a person's Natural Skill Set, Passions, and Purpose make them ideally suited.

Career Risks—Risks such as pursuing job changes, taking on new responsibilities, or seeking promotions.

Chosen Risk—A risk a person has determined is required for them to function. Such determination is not necessarily a result of conscious assessment.

Comfort Threshold—The limit of a person's Comfort Zone. Moving beyond the Comfort Threshold will take a person out of their Comfort Zone. On the Spectrum of All Risks, the Comfort Threshold is the point between Optional Risks and Avoided Risks.

Comfort Zone—The realm within which a person feels comfortable functioning.

Compound Rewards—The rewards that cannot be identified when a risk is being considered. As a result, they are the surprise rewards.

Creative Risks—Risks such as painting, drawing, taking on a writing challenge, or pursuing an unconventional design.

Direct Rewards—The rewards that can be identified when a risk is being considered and as a result will strongly influence the decision as to whether to take the risk.

Disaster Check—One of the finals steps in the risk assessment and success enhancement process. The Disaster Check involves evaluating the acceptability of any undesirable outcomes. A wholly unacceptable outcome dictates a decision not to proceed and hence avoid a "disaster."

Dream Job—A job that fully engages a person's Natural Skill Set and Passions.

Emotional Fear—A fear that is gut driven and instinctive but not necessarily based on fact. The alternative is a Mental Fear that is mind driven, rational, and based on fact.

Emotional Risks—Risks that require a person to be emotionally vulnerable.

Financial Risks—A person's risk tolerance in activities such as investing, borrowing, and lending money.

Gift of Mortality—A person's awareness and resulting actions based on the knowledge that their life is of finite duration.

Improved Likelihood—The revised chances expressed as a percentage of a certain outcome after POSEMs (Possibility of Success Enhancement Measures) are taken into account. (See Initial Likelihood.)

Initial Likelihood—The chances expressed as a percentage of a certain outcome before POSEMs (Possibility of Success Enhancement Measures) are taken into account. (See Improved Likelihood.)

Intellectual Risks—Risks such as a person's willingness to study a difficult topic, pursue information that challenges their convictions, or read an intellectually challenging book.

Intermediate Outcome—A Possible Outcome from a risk that falls between the Best Case and the Worst Case Outcome.

Invalid Fear—A fear that is not supported by facts or circumstances and is as a result is invalid.

Life Structure—The extent to which a person incorporates their Natural Skill Set, Passions, Purpose, Calling into their day-to-day life.

Mental Fear—A fear that is mind driven, rational, and based on fact. The alternative is an Emotional Fear that is gut driven and instinctive but not necessarily based on fact.

Natural Skill Set—An assessment of a person's innate abilities as they are sorted into three categories based on ability and level of fulfillment. The three categories are Strengths, Serviceable Skills, and Areas for Improvement or Weaknesses.

Opportunity Territory—The area beyond a person's Comfort Zone in which they will find opportunities they have not yet taken. On the Spectrum of All Risks, the Opportunity Territory is the area to the right of the line between Optional Risks and Avoided Risks.

Optional Risk—A risk a person has decided to take even though is not required for them to function.

Passion—A person's deeply held desires, concerns, and beliefs.

Passion/Life Nexus—The extent to which a person has brought their Passions and their Life Structure into alignment.

Perceived Risk—The perceived level of risk without risk mitigation and success enhancement measures taken into account. The same risk when revised by taking proposed risk mitigation and success enhancement actions into account is the Actual Risk.

Personal Risk Inclination—A person's self-assessed risk inclination ranked on a scale of 1 to 10 with 1 being very risk averse and 10 being very risk inclined.

Physical Risks—Activities that involve some risk of injury such as riding a motorcycle, river rafting, rock climbing, or skydiving.

Possible Outcome—An outcome that could result from a certain course of action.

Possible Outcomes Matrix—A matrix that contains all possible outcomes being assessed in order from most to least desirable with the corresponding likelihood of each possible outcome presented as a percentage.

POSEMs (Possibility of Success Enhancement Measures)—Actions that can improve the chances of a desirable outcome and reduce the chances of an undesirable outcome when applied to a certain course of action.

Purpose—A person's perception of their reason for being.

RQ—A numerical indication of a person's current risk inclination over a broad range of risk types that is derived by self-assessment. RQs fall between 1 and 10 with 1 being very risk averse and 10 being very risk inclined.

RASE (Risk Assessment/Success Enhancement Tool)—An eight-step tool for evaluating and deciding on a certain course of action that includes identifying possible outcomes and actions that can increase the chances of positive results. The RASE tool is available at *www.TakeRisks.com/tools*.

Reality Check—Assessing the validity of fears that are resulting from a possible course of action.

Relationship Risks—Risks such as a willingness to pursue a new relationship, spend time with someone despite an uncertain outcome, or make a relationship commitment.

Research POSEMs—Research that can increase the chances of a risk yielding a positive outcome and decrease the chances of a negative outcome. (See POSEMs.)

Risk—Any action with an undetermined outcome.

Serviceable Skills—One of three categories into which a person's capabilities are sorted in determining their Natural Skill Set. Serviceable Skills are the tasks and skills for which ability is high but fulfillment is low. The other two categories are Strengths and Areas for Improvement or Weaknesses.

Social Risks—Risks such as a person introducing themself to someone they don't know or putting themself in an unfamiliar social situation even at the risk of possible embarrassment.

Spectrum of All Risks—A graphic representation of the Spectrum of All Risks a person can contemplate, ranging from the least risky actions on the left to the most risky actions on the right. The risk categories on the spectrum fit into one of three categories; Chosen, Optional, and Avoided.

Spiritual Risks—A person's willingness to place their trust in concepts that may be unproveable or that they do not fully understand.

Strength/Weakness Paradox—The premise that a positive trait, if applied in the extreme, can become negative. A Strength Optimization exercise that facilitates applying this concept is available at *www.TakeRisks.com/tools*.

Strengths—One of three categories into which a person's capabilities are sorted in determining their Natural Skill Set. Strengths are the tasks and skills for which both ability and fulfillment are high. The other two categories are Serviceable Skills and Areas for Improvement or Weaknesses.

Turning Points—Significant events that change the direction of a person's life. A Turning Point exercise that facilitates applying this concept is available at *www.TakeRisks.com/tools*.

Unsupported Fear—A fear that is not supported by facts or circumstances and is as a result unsupportable.

Valid Fear—A fear that is supported by facts or circumstances and is as a result valid.

Weaknesses—One of three categories into which a person's capabilities are sorted in determining their Natural Skill Set. Weaknesses are the tasks and skills for which both ability and fulfillment are low. The other two categories are Strengths and Serviceable Skills. (Also see Areas for Improvement.)

Worst Case Outcome—The least desirable outcome that can result from a certain course of action.

Endnotes

[1] SRBI Public Affairs for *Time Magazine,* survey of 1,009 adult Americans conducted by telephone December 13–14, 2004, published January 17, 2005.

[2] Post, Thierry, Martijn J. Van den Assem, Guido Baltussen, and Richard H. Thaler, "Deal or No Deal? Decision Making Under Risk in a Large-Payoff Game Show" (Tinbergen Institute Discussion Paper, June 2007).

[3] National Public Radio, All Things Considered Commentary: "Dying of Cancer," March 10, 2004.

[4] Barsky, Robert, Thomas Juster, Miles Kimball, and Matthew Shapiro. "Preference Parameters and Behavioral Heterogeneity: An Experimental Approach in the Health and Retirement Study." *Quarterly Journal of Economics*, Vol. 112: 537–579. MIT Press. May 1997.

[5] Ibid.

[6]   Ball-Rokeach, Sandra, Milton Rokeach, and Joel Grube. "The Great American Values Test." *Psychology Today.* November 1984.

[7]   Ibid.

[8]   Spinks, Sarah. "Inside the Teenage Brain." *Frontline.* PBS. January 31, 2002.

[9]   Alliance for Human Research Protection (*www.ahrp.org*). "Brain Development & Teen Mood Swings." ABC, Sunday, August 24, 2003.

[10]   Spinks, Sarah. "Inside the Teenage Brain." *Frontline.* PBS. January 31, 2002.

[11]   Wallis, Claudia. "The New Science of Happiness." *Time Magazine.* January 17, 2005.

[12]   Neighmond, Patricia. "Study Finds Most Israelis are Affected by Middle East Conflict, But Tend to Develop Tolerance to the Violence." Morning Edition, National Public Radio, August 6, 2003. *www.npr.org/ programs/morning/transcripts/2003/aug/030806.neighmond.html.*

[13]   Historic information on shark attacks in Hawaii is available at:

www.hawaii.gov/dlnr/dar/sharks/incidents.html
www.hawaii.gov/dlnr/dar/sharks/stateincidents.html, and
www.hawaii.gov/dlnr/dar/sharks/images/Maui04.jpg

Information on how to avoid shark attacks can be found many places on the Internet including *www.hawaii.gov/dlnr/dar/sharks/dosdonts.html.*

[14]   Kluger, Jeffrey. "Why we worry about the things we shouldn't and ignore the things we should." *Time Magazine.* December 4, 2006, pp. 66–67.

[15]   Schüz, Jacobsen, et al. "Cellular Telephone Use and Cancer Risk: Update of a Nationwide Danish Cohort." *Journal of the National Cancer Institute.* Volume 98, Number 23. December, 2006.

[16] Various Sources: Ropeik, David and George Gray, Ph.D. *Risk—A Practical Guide for Deciding What's Really Safe and What's Really Dangerous in the World Around You*. Harvard Center for Risk Analysis, Harvard School of Public Health. Houghton Mifflin Co., 2002; National Ski Areas Association; National Sporting Goods Association (*Sports Participation*, 2003 edition); National Safety Council (*Injury Facts*, 2002 and 2003 editions).

[17] Odds of Death Due to Injury, United States, 2003. National Safety Council, a membership organization dedicated to protecting life and promoting health. *www.NSC.org*. August 2, 2006.

[18] Ropeik, David and George Gray, Ph.D. *Risk—A Practical Guide for Deciding What's Really Safe and What's Really Dangerous in the World Around You*. Harvard Center for Risk Analysis, Harvard School of Public Health. Houghton Mifflin Co., 2002. pp. 299–300.

[19] Treasurer, Bill. "How Risk-Taking Really Works." *Training Magazine*. January 2000.

[20] Kluger, Jeffrey. "Why we worry about the things we shouldn't and ignore the things we should." *Time Magazine*. December 4, 2006, p. 67.

Index